Cover design: Jason Pearson

© 2019, ECFAPress

ISBN: 978-1-949365-19-1

CONTENTS

Contents

Contents

APPRECIATION

In our first book, *Lessons From the Nonprofit Boardroom*, Dan thanked the leaders, board chairs, and board members that served in ECFA member ministries. John thanked the long-suffering board chairs who endured his 30 years as a ministry CEO.

For this book, we consulted with our closest advisors (Claudette Busby and Joanne Pearson!) and they suggested we express appreciation to all of the board members we have served with over these many years. Of course, Claudette and Joanne realized this would be a very, very long list—so rather than listing every name, we're noting what we've learned from this very special group.

Even now, we seek to be lifelong learners—and it's a rare board meeting when we don't reflect on (shall we say), "The Good, The Bad, and The Ugly" lessons learned in the board-room. Here are seven insights we've gleaned from the men and women we've served with:

☑ Many of our board colleagues believe—deeply—in the power of prayer. We've learned to trust God more.

☑ As CEOs, both of us have been blessed with wise board chairs. We've learned that the wrong board chair and/or the wrong agenda—can create sleepless nights.

☑ We've seen board members prioritize board meeting attendance at great personal sacrifice. We've learned that faithful attendance generates profound goodwill.

☑ We've also endured board members who were knee-deep in the operational weeds—much to everyone's chagrin. We've learned that savvy board chairs are the best antidote to board members who want to micromanage the ministry.

☑ We've appreciated spouses of board members who joyfully prioritize their family's charitable giving to these organizations. We've learned that this expectation must be crystal clear before people are invited onto the board— and spouses must concur.

☑ We are stunned (and blessed!) by how frequently some board members becomes trusted friends. We've learned to be more people-focused versus agenda-focused.

☑ We also readily admit that we write and teach about board governance much better than we practice it! We've learned that trusting God—in all things—is more powerful than orchestrating board meetings in our own strength.

We've learned so much from all of our board member colleagues—and we're grateful. We wish we could salute each and every one of you by name. But please know that your service has inspired us in so many under-the-radar ways over the years. You have touched our lives and added to our governance understanding.

Thank you!

INTRODUCTION

Apparently, board members and CEOs have more questions about board governance.

We mistakenly assumed that after writing *Lessons From the Nonprofit Boardroom* and *Lessons From the Church Boardroom* (each with 40 short chapters), that 80 lessons would have covered the governance waterfront. Apparently not.

So we'll keep at it—and now we humbly present *More Lessons From the Nonprofit Boardroom* with another 40 short chapters. Like you, we seek to honor God as lifelong learners. And when we talk with ministry board members, we listen and learn—and three themes have recently emerged:

Effectiveness, Excellence, Elephants!

❑ **EFFECTIVENESS.** As stewards of God's work, board members certainly want to be effective. Yet would your board agree on what effectiveness looks like in your boardroom? In *More Lessons*, you'll find helpful chapters on how to eliminate fuzziness between board and staff roles, the power of "big rock" agenda items, and why dashboards are not the secret solution to effectiveness.

You'll also find a bonus lesson (see page 221) on how to leverage ECFA's new online board self-assessment tool, NonprofitBoardScore™. Your board members can complete the self-assessment and receive immediate feedback on six

NonprofitBoardScore™

critical governance elements including: Spiritual Atmosphere, Board-CEO Synergy, Intentionality, Faithful Administration, Structure and Style, and Culture.

❑ **EXCELLENCE.** Perhaps you've seen the Dilbert coffee mug with this definition: "Excellence: An abstract goal that's whatever you're not doing now." (Too true!)

Tom Peters, apparently, also received more questions after co-authoring *In Search of Excellence* in 1982. So in 2018 he wrote *The Excellence Dividend.* Here's how he defines excellence:

> I believe—oh, how deeply I believe—that excellence is far more than just an organizing business principle that can be reduced to a series of "success traits." Excellence can be the way we live our lives, professional as well as personal, the way we support one another, particularly in difficult times. Excellence is the seemingly small acts that shout, "We care," and which linger in the memories of those we interact with—our own people, our communities, our suppliers, our customers.[1]

But is excellence an appropriate aspiration for the Christ-centered boardroom? Absolutely! At Holy Trinity Brompton (HTB) in London, the church leadership affirms four core values: excellence, serving others, friendliness, and fun. Nicky Gumbel, HTB's vicar, says they "aim for perfection but settle for excellence."

God has blessed that focus. *Alpha*, the no-pressure course exploring the Christian faith (now taught in 169 countries in 112 languages), was launched at HTB. Interestingly, the church describes their culture as "a sailboat where everyone on board had an active role to play, versus a cruise ship where passengers were served but never served others."[2]

So what would excellence in your boardroom look like? It might have the taste and feel of Eric Liddell's inspirational line in *Chariots of Fire* (see Lesson 11), "When I run, I feel His pleasure." When your board members serve, do they feel God's pleasure?

❏ **ELEPHANTS!** In dozens of hallways outside boardrooms, we've listened patiently as board members enumerated their board meeting horror stories. One common theme: *few board chairs have the intestinal fortitude to address the elephant in the boardroom.*

We know. We know. It takes courage and as Jeffrey Sonnenfeld notes, "almost no one wants to be a skunk at a lawn party." This governance guru believes that board members "are, almost without exception, intelligent, accomplished and comfortable with power. But if you put them into a group that discourages dissent, they nearly always start to conform. The ones that don't often self-select out."[3]

So how should your board counteract this tendency to let sleeping dogs lie? (*Whew! That's our third animal metaphor. Sorry!*)

To address the elephant in the room, you must have the right board members in the room. Board service is not for the weak of heart. So in these lessons, you'll find numerous alerts, cautions, and warnings: how to guard your CEO's soul, insights on succession planning, the *Governance Pendulum Principle*, the dangers of botched executive sessions, and why resumé-builders make lousy board members.

We pray that this book will be a catalyst for your board to have numerous healthy conversations about effectiveness, excellence, and elephants. And we also salute you and thank you for accepting the sacred trust of ministry board service. God is honored.

Dan Busby
Winchester, Virginia

John Pearson
San Clemente, California

P.S. As in our previous books, we've changed most of the board member names and places to protect the innocent (and the guilty)—and the content of several lessons delivers major hints about the author. (Dan or John? Guess!) You'll also find references to practical tools and templates that will enrich your board meetings.

To access 22 downloadable tools, order the new resource:

ECFA Tools and Templates for Effective Board Governance: Time-Saving Solutions for Your Board

PART 1:

THE POWERFUL IMPACT
OF HIGHLY ENGAGED BOARDS

The first responsibility of a leader is to define reality.
The second is to say thank you.
In between the two,
the leader must become a servant and a debtor.[1]

Max De Pree

1 | BIG BLESSINGS ABOUND WHEN GOVERNANCE FAITHFULNESS FLOURISHES

Two stories: "The Board and the Bachelor Farmer" and "$1.5 Billion Worth of Burger Blessings!"

We come up with our own big, hairy, audacious targets and expect God to bless and fund them. However, just because a goal is so big it can only be accomplished if God shows up does not mean it aligns with His will.[1]

Gary G. Hoag, R. Scott Rodin, and Wesley K. Willmer

Observing a board meeting several years ago (you can learn many things by listening and not talking), I noticed the uneasy body language around the room after the CEO concluded his board report with, "And now I'd like to read a letter we received this week from an attorney."

Most of us grimaced. That can't be good!

But the glass-half-full folks were right. The lawyer's letter announced—out of the blue—that a bachelor farmer had died, and enclosed was an estate gift for the ministry. The organization was small, but the unrestricted gift was large—more than $275,000!

Ironically, earlier in the meeting, after a team member had reported on some stunning Kingdom results, the board launched into the Doxology in four-part harmony:

> Praise God from whom
> all blessings flow!

A second rendering of the Doxology almost broke out.

At the end of the meeting, the board chair asked me to pray, and I was blessed with this Holy Spirit nudge to remind the board about governance faithfulness.

"Before I pray," I began, "think back a few years to when this bachelor farmer was deciding where to invest his estate gifts. Undoubtedly he did his research and concluded that your ministry was worthy of a large gift. But I'm guessing that back then, he also looked at the list of board members to discern if those men and women were faithful stewards of the ministry's mission, vision, programs, and funds.

"And today, I'm sure, as this bachelor farmer did, dozens of other givers are looking at your board—at your faithfulness—and discerning if your ministry is worthy of their giving. Board faithfulness, every day, every meeting, every year, counts for eternity."

Traveling home from that exhilarating meeting, I was reminded that big blessings abound when governance faithfulness and management faithfulness flourish.

For example, imagine the faithfulness factors that enabled Joan B. Kroc, wife of Ray Kroc, the founder of McDonald's

Corporation, to bless The Salvation Army with a gift in excess of $1.5 billion.[2]

The gift by Mrs. Kroc was designated for the development of community centers across the country, similar to the landmark Ray and Joan Kroc Corps Community Center in San Diego, California, that opened in June 2002.

Take note and make no mistake: Joan Kroc was not an uninvolved giver. Reports indicate that after the San Diego community center opened, she would often show up anonymously, sit unassumingly in the lobby, and observe this unique ministry to children, youth, and adults from the vantage point of a quiet visitor.

What did she see, hear, touch, and smell as a quiet philanthropist that birthed

"Board faithfulness, every day, every meeting, every year, counts for eternity."

the vision for replicating this community center experience across the country? Clearly she observed and experienced governance faithfulness and management faithfulness.

If you've been a board member or ministry leader or manager for more than a month, you know that governance faithfulness and management faithfulness don't come easily.

But also know this: boards of Christ-centered nonprofits are often enviable in their passion and commitment to the ministry. In ECFA's research of its members, 98 percent of board members "clearly see the board's work as Christ-centered," 98 percent "strive to conduct their work with Christ-centered character," and 96 percent agree with this statement: "It's very important that we know and leverage the God-given strengths of every board member."[3]

Every day, eight-hour shift after shift, a community center—
and virtually all ministries and churches—require team
members who give it all and more for Kingdom purposes.
You can't phone it in. Ministry management is in-the-
trenches and get-it-done work.

Let's replay the video on those days when Joan Kroc visited
her community center and ask ourselves: What if the restroom
cleaning team had said yesterday's cleaning was good enough?
What if a program director who had been up late with a client
emergency cancelled a program because "they owe me a
morning off"? What if an unruly fifth-grader got "what he
deserved" instead of love and compassion?

Praise the Lord—the team at the Ray and Joan Kroc Corps
Community Center in San Diego passed the test. Imagine the
hundreds of thousands of children, youth, and adults across
the nation who are now being ministered to by The Salvation
Army because faithful managers and administrators (and
board members!) up and down the line showed up and
prayerfully and thoughtfully executed their work, never
realizing they were on stage.

Look more closely behind every big blessing of God and
you'll likely find a small army of board members, managers
and administrators (faithful and fruitful stewards) who show
up every day ready for Kingdom opportunities.

Jesus said in Matthew 10:42, "This is a large work I've called
you into, but don't be overwhelmed by it. It's best to start
small. Give a cool cup of water to someone who is thirsty, for
instance. The smallest act of giving or receiving makes you a
true apprentice. You won't lose out on a thing" (MSG).

BOARDROOM LESSON

Faithfulness, every day, every meeting, every year, counts for eternity. As the board discerns direction, practices faithfulness, and prays for fruitfulness, God will determine the size and scope of the ministry's impact.

Board Action Steps:

○ **1. Read:** *The Choice: The Christ-Centered Pursuit of Kingdom Outcomes* by Gary G. Hoag, R. Scott Rodin, and Wesley K. Willmer.

○ **2. Inspire:** At your next meeting, inspire and motivate your board members with a compelling story of governance faithfulness.

○ **3. Discuss:** How do we monitor and evaluate governance and management faithfulness?

Prayer

Lord, help us to be faithful to the roles You have called us to in this ministry. May we be ever ready to pursue the Kingdom opportunities You set before us.
Amen.

2 | ENGAGE BOARD MEMBERS IN GENERATIVE THINKING

They rely on generative thinking in their day jobs but are rarely asked to think collaboratively in the boardroom.

Good governance is not just about doing work better; it's about ensuring your organization does better work.[1]

Bill Ryan

"They just lie to you. They'll tell you *anything* to persuade you to join the board. You say yes and—*presto!*—your name's on the website and you go to your first board meeting. But then it's too late! You realize that this board is just as dysfunctional as the last board you served on."

An experienced board member shared that sentiment with me recently. I nodded my head with empathy and thought about the insights from the helpful book *Governance as Leadership.*[2] The authors describe four governance scenarios, including three that are unhealthy. Next they introduce three modes of governance: fiduciary, strategic, and generative.[3] Then they lobby for a more mature approach to governance, which they label "Type III Governance"—a collaborative blend of all three. (And note that just one or two are not enough.)

Look at these scenarios and discern. Are you telling the truth to your board prospects?

Which Scenario Describes Your Board?[3]

Governance by Fiat is the first unhealthy scenario. That's when the board displaces staff. Sometimes the staff lacks competence or capacity so the board jumps in. Often the board enjoys staff work. Either way, it's dysfunctional.

Governance by Default is the second scenario. Both the board and the ministry executives disengage. No one has their eye on the governance ball, and the important work of governance is minimized. Left alone, you have a train wreck waiting to happen.

Leadership as Governance sounds good, but it's cockeyed. Here the ministry staff displace the board members. The CEO and/or senior team frequently make decisions that should be made by the board. This happens especially with founder-led organizations. Often the organization appears to be operating smoothly. Internally, this dysfunction never ends well. Sooner or later something will go awry.

Governance as Leadership is the only healthy scenario. Here the board and executives collaborate. Each understands their appropriate roles, but unlike most boards, the staff affirms the board members when they upgrade their engagement through generative thinking.

☑ 4 Governance Scenarios	Characteristics	Healthy?
❏ Governance by Fiat	The board displaces the staff.	No
❏ Governance by Default	Both the board and the staff disengage.	No
❏ Leadership as Governance	The CEO and staff displace the board.	No
❏ Governance as Leadership	The board and staff collaborate and leverage generative thinking.	YES

GOVERNANCE AS LEADERSHIP: THE GOVERNANCE TRIANGLE

How effective is your board in all three modes of governance? "When trustees work well in all three of these modes, the board achieves governance as leadership."[4]

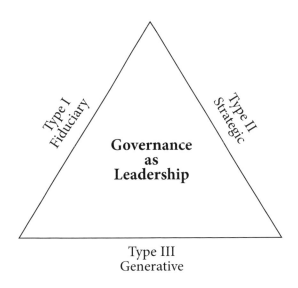

So what's "generative governance"? The authors use a variety of definitions to explain this cognitive process of boards that excel: sense-making, reflective practice, framing organizations, personal knowledge, etc. We like "sensible foolishness" the best.

The authors comment, "In their 'day jobs' as managers, professionals, or leaders of organizations, board members routinely rely on generative thinking, so much so they have no need to name it or analyze it. They just do it. But in the boardroom, trustees are at a double disadvantage. Most boards do not routinely practice generative thinking."[5]

> *No one has their eye on the governance ball—and the important work of governance is minimized. Left undone, it's a train wreck waiting to happen.*

They add, "When it comes to generative governing, most trustees add too little, too late."

Generative governance goes beyond "fiduciary governance" (Type I) and beyond "strategic governance" (Type II). This "Type III" approach typically involves three steps:

STEP 1: Noticing cues and clues. Different people can take the same data and arrive at different meanings.

STEP 2: Choosing and using frames. Understanding the "fuzzy front end" of a product development process, for example.

STEP 3: Thinking retrospectively. The counterintuitive high value of dwelling on the past to understand patterns that might impact the future.

> Generative thinking is essential to governing. As long as governing means what most people think it means—setting the goals and direction of an organization and holding management accountable for progress toward these goals— then generative thinking has to be essential to governing. Generative thinking is where goal-setting and direction-setting originate. The contributions boards make to mission-setting, strategy-development, and problem solving certainly shape organizations. But it is cues and frames, along with retrospective thinking, that enable the sense-making on which these other processes depend.[6]

Yikes! Think about this final zinger: "And a closer examination of nonprofits suggests something else: Although generative work is essential to governing, boards do very little of it."[7] Research affirms this statement for ECFA members as well.[8]

Imagine if one could serve on a board that wasn't dysfunctional. Imagine if it was a healthy board and the leadership leveraged the unique spiritual gifts, strengths, and passions of each board member. Imagine if one could serve on a Type III board and be a blessing to the board chair, the CEO, and the Kingdom. *Just imagine.*

BOARDROOM LESSON

Board members rely on generative thinking in their day jobs but are rarely asked to think collaboratively in the boardroom. Instead, create a governance triangle of the fiduciary roles and strategic roles of the board that are influenced and integrated into generative governance— the healthiest scenario!

Board Action Steps:

○ 1. **Read:** *Governance as Leadership: Reframing the Work of Nonprofit Boards* by Richard P. Chait, William P. Ryan, and Barbara E. Taylor.

○ 2. **Research:** Ask a board member to research and report on the concept of "generative thinking" and how it might be a tool for engaging the hearts and minds of every board member—and be a catalyst for making better decisions.

○ 3. **Explore:** What if, over the next 12 months, every board member became a "best practices scout" and observed a healthy board meeting at another ministry?

Prayer

Lord, You have blessed us with amazing men and
women who have incredible hearts and minds.
Teach us how to activate generative thinking
in the boardroom for Kingdom purposes.
Amen.

3 | THE PRODUCTIVITY PAYOFF OF INTENTIONAL HOSPITALITY

Create hospitable and productive board environments.

Hospitality has to do with equity for each member.
Enabling each to feel authentic and needed and worthwhile
is an act of hospitality.
The way we provide for the needs of the group
in the physical setting is part of this.[1]

Max De Pree

Renowned CEO, author, and board consultant Max De Pree shares the story of an English visitor who watched his first American football game and observed, "The game combines the two worst elements of American culture—violence and committee meetings."[2]

Fortunately, in our many years of board service and observing boards in action, violence has rarely been a part of the equation! However, when boards fail to take the time and effort to nurture a hospitable and productive environment in the boardroom, the higher calling of the board to Kingdom-oriented, mission-focused governance can naturally become lost. The result: a sea of committee jockeying, structural red tape, and operational overstepping.

Here's what happens when intentional hospitality is minimized:

- We know a CEO who, seeking to save money, had scheduled a board meeting at the ministry's office—instead of a more conducive off-site environment. Unfortunately, the meeting had constant distractions and disappointments: phones ringing, "emergency" requests for the CEO, and piecemeal refreshments. *Cheaper—yes. Effective—no.*

- At another ministry, Marianna was new to the board and relatively new to board service in general. The staff provided her the board materials in plenty of time, but in a completely different order from the way they were addressed in the agenda. She spent most of her first meeting flipping back and forth in an attempt to be on the same page (literally!) with the rest of the board.

> *When boards fail to take the time and effort to nurture a hospitable and productive environment in the boardroom, the higher calling of the board to Kingdom-oriented, mission-focused governance can become lost.*

- *And here's another hospitality mishap!* Even though Simeon had already served three years on the board, he'd never had a one-on-one conversation with the board chair—other than those awkward elevator conversations. *Imagine!* Consequently, the chair was unaware that Simeon's wife had successfully battled cancer last year or that Simeon's new book on leadership was arriving in a month. In fact, Simeon was deeply disappointed that neither the board chair nor the CEO had connected the dots between

Simeon's personal and professional life and his board service.

- *Here's one more example—void of intentional hospitality.* At this board meeting, the agenda was jam-packed, but the board chair and the CEO inappropriately crowded the first hours with routine business. *Yawn!* Thus, the most critical agenda topics were crammed into the final hour—just before dinner. You've seen this before at ill-planned board meetings—*the deer in the headlights look*!

So how can the CEO and board chair nurture an environment of hospitality that leads to productive, meaningful, and impactful governance? The spiritual gift of hospitality, according to author Bruce Bugbee, is "the divine enablement to care for people by providing fellowship, food, and shelter."[3] It is important to discern who on your board or staff is specially enabled by God to practice hospitality—and invite that person to help you create a warm and inviting board meeting environment.

Called to Serve: Creating and Nurturing the Effective Volunteer Board by Max De Pree offers a plethora of gems for creating an ideal boardroom environment. Here are six practical takeaways:

1. **Design the agenda on the bell curve.** "I have found it very helpful to think about designing an agenda by following the lines of a bell curve," says De Pree. He adds, "At the top of the curve (that's my shorthand for the way energy at board meetings starts out slowly, then rises, then declines) for regular board meetings we will want to focus on the future and plan time to be thorough."[4]

Keeping critical agenda items in the high energy part of the meeting ensures meaningful engagement. This includes topics such as significant issues, vexing problems, and key appointments. De Pree also emphasizes the need to prioritize time to dream, time to strategize for the future, and we would add, always give top billing to prayer.

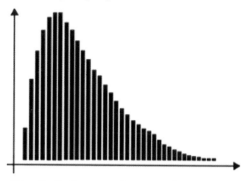

The Bell Curve of a Board Meeting

2. **Nurture strong personal relationships.** De Pree writes, "Many people seem to feel that a good board structure enables high performance. This is simply not so. What's crucial is the quality of our personal relationships. The [board chair] and the [CEO] set the tone for good relationships, but it is up to every individual on the board to develop, nurture, and polish good relationships. While we want to do a good job of structuring the board's work, good working relationships are more important."[5]

3. **Work seriously at the growth, needs, and potential of board members.** "The environment we create for growth and potential, as well as the satisfactions that come from doing good work well, motivate good people to work for

love. I have always thought about board members as perpetual volunteers. The best of them are like lifetime free agents." De Pree continues: "Because the best board members have many opportunities and choices, the organization and its leaders develop programs for the care and feeding of these vital volunteers. They are provided good orientation and lucid, succinct information. There are ways for them to understand and become intimate with the work of the organization."[6]

4. **Work seriously at the growth, needs, and potential of the CEO.** Christ-centered boards should inspire their CEOs to thrive by providing an adequate budget and time for personal and professional growth. This includes giving the CEO "space" to be creative in his or her role, while also helping him or her to set priorities.[7] When the board cares about the CEO's growth—and the CEO cares about the growth of team members—there will be a direct relationship between personal growth and organizational growth.

5. **Say "thank you creatively."** De Pree describes a creative thank you gift given to Kareem Abdul-Jabbar, the seven-foot, two-inch pro basketball player, during his last season with the Los Angeles Lakers. "In Dallas, a business-man presented a gift to Kareem and had obviously thought about saying thank you. He had a special table built, higher than usual, on which to place the gift for Kareem. The businessman observed that you shouldn't ever make a person stoop to receive a gift. Now I think that is a marvelous lesson, isn't it?"[8]

How does your board thank people? Do you consider the recipient's "love language?"

6. **Carry on Max De Pree's legacy of being a servant.** Max De Pree was called home to his Savior in August 2017. De Pree left a legacy of vast knowledge and wisdom about leadership and management, always emphasizing putting people first. Arguably one of De Pree's most lasting messages is one highlighted by Fuller Seminary (where he served as board chair) in its tribute to De Pree: "The first responsibility of a leader is to define reality. The second is to say thank you. In between the two, the leader must become a servant and a debtor."[9]

In our book *Lessons From the Nonprofit Boardroom*, we introduced the concept of taking "10 Minutes for Governance" in every meeting—to remind board members that good governance does not happen by osmosis (Lesson 39).[10] We suggest you invest 10 minutes for governance at your next meeting to think more intentionally about boardroom hospitality. Our prediction: if you approach the topic with God-honoring humility and servanthood, you'll see an immediate payoff in board meeting productivity.

BOARDROOM LESSON

Highly effective boards do not leave the boardroom environment to its own natural devices and distractions. Instead, the best boards intentionally nurture hospitality which enhances productivity.

Board Action Steps:

○ **1. Assign:** Give each board member a copy of *Called to Serve: Creating and Nurturing the Effective Volunteer Board* by Max De Pree. Assignment: bring one idea to the next meeting for nurturing the boardroom environment.

○ **2. Analyze:** Give some thought to the energy and focus level of your board meetings. Do they fit the "bell curve" pattern? Maximize your agenda to place critical items, including prayer, into the high energy segments of the meeting.

○ **3. Appoint:** Who on your staff or board has the spiritual gift of hospitality? Invite that person to help you create a more hospitable and productive environment for your board meetings.

○ **4. Anticipate:** Expect that not every board member will read De Pree's book (even though it is just 91 pages!). So email everyone the link to the index of 30 short blogs highlighting 30 key topics from *Called to Serve.*[11] Visit: *http://ecfagovernance.blogspot.com/2017/10/called-to-serve-no-board-detail-is-too.html*.

Prayer
Lord, help us to be intentional in the environment
we create for our board. May we be hospitable,
welcoming, and nurturing so that the board works
effectively for Your purposes and Your glory.
Amen.

4 | GUARDING YOUR CEO'S SOUL

Wise boards invest time—up front—to ensure their CEO's soul is not neglected.

Jesus indicates that it is possible to gain the world but lose your own soul. If He were talking to us as Christian leaders today, He might point out that it is possible to gain the world of ministry success and lose your own soul in the midst of it all. He might remind us that it is possible to find your soul, after so much seeking, only to lose it again.[1]

Ruth Haley Barton

The ministry is growing. The Great Commandment is being lived out in the organization and the Great Commission is being fulfilled.

The respect for and the popularity of the CEO has grown with each year of service. Still, you have a gnawing sense of wonderment, that little question in the back of your mind, the one you wish would go away—is it possible the soul of the CEO is being neglected? And what about the board? With everything going great on the surface, what about the state of the souls of the board members?

Let's start by defining soul care. A spiritual director and friend, Jenni Hoag, describes soul care as "thoughtful and careful attention to the inner being of the individual."[2] When the board and the CEO give attention to their souls by engaging in practices that enrich themselves spiritually, it positions them for proper interaction with those on staff, volunteers, and the greater community. When they don't, well, that's when the wheels can come off fast.

How does a board address this topic? Not often enough, according to ECFA research.[3] Many boards have never discussed it. Others would not know how to bring it up. It's challenging because factors on the outside are easier to assess. We can see if someone is caring for their body by getting adequate rest, taking time to exercise, enjoying vacation time regularly, and eating healthily to stay in good physical condition. It is far more difficult to discern whether or not someone is attending to their inner being by spending time reading the Scriptures, praying, or simply enjoying solitude with God on a regular basis.

In many cases, soul care does not make the board agenda until a crisis happens. A staff member might blow the whistle on verbal, emotional, physical, or sexual abuse. An internet filter may reveal that the CEO is struggling with pornography. These are just a few tragic examples.

Other symptoms often linked to the need for soul care include (but are not limited to): marriage conflict, outbursts of anger, selfish inclinations, and any behavior that appears to exhibit a desire for power or control. Spiritual directors see these tendencies as warning lights that a person's inner being needs care.

These crisis examples and symptoms sober us to the reality that any ministry is susceptible to spiritual problems. Many could be avoided with special attention to soul care.

Today's culture is one where men and women work together, volunteer together, eat together, and perhaps travel together—moreover, they serve together. In our individual and collective ministry efforts, we must do

> *"As the CEO goes,*
> *so goes the ministry.*
> *And, as the soul goes,*
> *so goes the CEO."*

what is right before God and every person, being sure that we bring honor to Jesus Christ.

How can the board ensure that Jesus Christ is being honored in all relationships and interactions? *Very simply, it cannot.* But the board can live out and promote the "one another" teachings of the Scriptures. The board can demonstrate a "beyond reproach" culture that celebrates biblical integrity and godliness by its words and actions. The board can set and uphold high standards that invite the trust of staff, the board, and a watching world.

Attending to soul care is one way the board can foster a "beyond reproach" culture. As our colleague Stephen Macchia says, "As the CEO goes, so goes the ministry. And, as the soul goes, so goes the CEO."[4] The psalmist reminds us to pay attention to the soul when he says, "Search me, O God, and know my heart; test me and know my anxious thoughts. Point out anything in me that offends You and lead me along the path of everlasting life" (Psalm 139:23-24 NLT). When the soul of the CEO or the souls of the board members are neglected, the organization is in for trouble. It's like a teenager running through a fireworks factory with a lit blowtorch. It isn't *whether* something is going to blow up—it's just a matter of *when*.[5]

Various conditions may signal that the board, the CEO, or staff members have neglected soul care. Conditions might include: a sense of isolation, abuse of authority, setting unreasonable expectations in reporting relationships, a competitive attitude, an independent spirit, or a lack of accountability. There are two major warning signals of a troubled soul:

- **Lack of humility.** The measure of a CEO's humility is a true barometer of the soul. Andrew Murray notes that without humility "there can be no true abiding in God's presence, abiding faith, or love or joy or strength. Humility is the only soil in which the graces root; the lack of humility is the sufficient explanation of every defect and failure."[6] This is why the lack of humility rates as the number one warning signal.

- **Self-interest.** CEOs must pursue God and focus on abiding in Christ. A major warning sign is when a leader places self-interest ahead of the things of God and the needs of the ministry, evidenced in arrogant language and prideful behavior. You will often hear a spiritually healthy CEO say, "I serve as CEO," not "I am the CEO"—a subtle but profound indicator of their motivation.

Ralph Enlow warns, "Celebrity will seduce you before you know it. If you have to self-promote in order to get the opportunities you seek, you are selling out. Your capacity to move people toward God will be slowly supplanted by your ambition."[7] Dallas Willard adds, "The blind pride of putting oneself at the center of the universe is the hinge upon which the entire world of the ruined self turns. When we are lost to God, we are also lost to ourselves."[8] Board members must hold one another and the CEO accountable for engaging in spiritual practices that reflect the pursuit of God and abiding in Christ.

What are meaningful ways that boards and CEOs may engage on soul care considerations? Adapted from the writings of Stephen Macchia, here are some possible topics:[9]

1. Encourage the CEO to have both a day off and a Sabbath each week. "On the seventh day, He rested" (Gen. 2:2 NIV). The comment made by Moses in Exodus 31:17 is even more enlightening: "In six days the Lord made heaven and earth, but on the seventh day He ceased from labor, and was refreshed." He refreshed himself. The soul is not well without rest. John Ortberg reminds us that when your soul is at rest, "your will is undivided and obeys God with joy. Your mind has thoughts of truth and beauty. You desire what is wholesome and good."[10]

2. Encourage the CEO to be at home more nights during the week than out for ministry responsibilities. Ignore this rule of thumb at the peril of the organization. When leaders invest and enjoy quality time with their spouses and children, this God-honoring priority will be observed and replicated by others.

3. Encourage the CEO to take his or her full vacation time each year—uninterrupted.

4. Encourage the CEO to have friends, both inside and outside the ministry, and to take time to cultivate healthy friendships.

5. Encourage the CEO to have daily time in the Word, prayer, and reflection.

6. Encourage the CEO to follow best practices for personal accountability. Do your board and CEO agree on what is appropriate when there are closed-door meetings and/or travel involving just two people?

7. Encourage the CEO to take time for his or her soul on retreat, away from the fray of busyness, and find spacious, uncluttered time to rest in God (ideally in a setting conducive to soul care).

8. Encourage the CEO to have hobbies and interests outside of the work of the ministry. There is "life" to be lived, and it's not all about the "work" of the organization!

9. Encourage the CEO to pursue both self-care (body) and soul-care (spirit).

10. Encourage the CEO to have a team that pursues the same soul care priorities.

Pride, self-centered leadership, sexual misconduct, narcissistic behavior,[11] and abuse in all its forms are sins as old as sin itself. As we find ourselves in an increasingly self-absorbed, over-sexualized, controlling culture where incidents of moral failures—though still relatively rare in Christ-centered ministries—make headlines with devastating effects, there is simply no room for this iniquity in our organizations. Boards can help create a "beyond reproach" culture by attending to the care of their own souls as well as the soul of the CEO and the ministry staff.

BOARDROOM LESSON

Boards and CEOs that prioritize soul care
will not prevent all crisis situations from happening,
but they can, in many cases, help their leaders
steer clear of spiritual disasters. In so doing,
they also preserve God's honor and reputation
and position the communities they serve
for vibrant spiritual growth.

Board Action Steps:

○ 1. **Read:** Ask one or more board members to read *Broken and Whole: A Leader's Path to Spiritual Transformation* by Stephen A. Macchia[12] and *Soul Keeping* by John Ortberg.

○ 2. **Evaluate:** Discuss with your CEO the 10 steps for soul care listed in this lesson. How is he or she doing with taking time for soul care?

○ 3. **Watch:** Be ever vigilant as a board for warning signs in ministry leaders such as self-interest or a lack of humility.

Prayer
Lord, help us care for our leaders so that they may
continue to bring glory to You, and so that our
ministry can be "blameless and innocent, children
of God without blemish in the midst of a crooked
and twisted generation" (Philippians 2:15 ESV).
Amen.

PART 2:

BOARDROOM TOOLS
AND TEMPLATES

If you want to teach people a new way of thinking,
don't bother trying to teach them.
Instead, give them a tool, the use of which
will lead to new ways of thinking.[1]

R. Buckminster Fuller

5 | DASHBOARDS ARE NOT A SECRET SAUCE FOR SOUND GOVERNANCE

Too often the use of dashboards does not clearly communicate the past and give signals for the future.

*Not everything that can be counted counts
and not everything that counts can be counted.*

"The dashboard that our board received from staff was very attractive. But with little context, we barely knew where we had been, and not much about where we were going," one ministry board member said.

Ministries accumulate massive amounts of data. Some data is useful for dashboard presentations; most is not. Ralph Waldo Emerson's words ring clear: "There are many things of which a wise man might wish to be ignorant."[1]

Well-chosen data can tell a story. Are key measurements up, down, or at a plateau? Is the ministry healthy—not just financially—but in other key ways? What is the status of the CEO's top five annual goals?

The starting point for measurement is not how creatively data can be presented. Effective dashboards begin with deciding which data elements—often called Key Performance

Indicators (KPIs)—are most important for your ministry. (See the Rockefeller Habits Checklist, No. 9.[2]) As businessman and board chair Max De Pree so aptly put it, "In my experience a failure to make a conscious decision about what it is we're going to measure often causes discombobulation and a lack of effectiveness and a lack of achievement."[3]

It takes data to create dashboards. *Data requires simplification—generally by humans.* And data becomes information only when it is shared in context. I will explain.

Let's take a number—103, for example.

If 103 is the batting average of a bullpen pitcher, it is good. If 103 is the fielding average of your starting right fielder, that is bad.

"In my experience a failure to make a conscious decision about what it is we're going to measure often causes discombobulation and a lack of effectiveness and a lack of achievement."

If 103 is the annual percentage of the health insurance cost increase for your organization, that is good. If 103 is the body temperature of your one-year-old child, that is bad.

Without context, 103 means nothing. And, without context, dashboards are meaningless.

SEVEN DASHBOARD QUESTIONS. To generate effective dashboard information, ministries should answer the following questions:

1. What data elements should be included in our dashboards?

2. Do we have the sophistication to generate effective dashboards from our IT system?

3. How can we reflect non-financial information in dashboards?

4. How often should we prepare dashboards?

5. Are we providing the proper level of context to explain the dashboards?

6. Do our dashboards tell a meaningful story?

7. Are we using the best dashboard presentation approach for our ministry?

Ministries should address all seven of these questions, *but a mistake in answering #7 is a dealbreaker!* Read on.

Our bookshelves are stocked with nearly every text written in recent years on the subject of dashboard reporting. The authors of these books wax eloquent on how to prepare every kind of dashboards imaginable—bar graphs, line graphs, dot plots, bullet graphs, sparklines, box plots, scatter plots, spatial maps, and much more. There are thousands of pages in these books that explain good dashboards and the bad—but all using graphical representations.

Here is the essence of what we have learned from the dashboard literature: Most of the dashboard guidance is designed for large organizations, with high-end software that can generate dashboards by sophisticated graph designers. We have found scant useable information for the modest-sized organization.

So, we believe the question isn't whether to dashboard or not. The question is whether to dashboard *using* or *not using* graphs. While the use of graphs from time-to-time is certainly not discouraged, we are convinced that most ministries are well-served to simplify their presentations using red, yellow and green dashboard signals and a columnar template approach.

Data becomes information only when it is connected to its context.

Using a simple template concept like the one shown below, board members will quickly turn their attention to the areas needing attention and celebrate with staff where progress has been made. The use of Red/Yellow/Green helps the board interpret the material, and the inclusion of prior information provides even more context on the topic.

We have just included a few sample metrics in these examples. In our book, *ECFA Tools and Templates for Effective Board Governance*,[4] expanded examples are shown and the templates shown on the following pages are downloadable so you can create your own metrics to use with this template.

1. Finance

	Target	6 months ago	Now
Days of operating cash on hand[1]	90 days	65 days	18 days
Net surplus or deficit YTD compared with YTD budget	Within 100K or better	$142,500 worse than budget	$102,000 worse than budget-to-date
Borrowing of temporarily restricted net assets	0	0	$200,000

[1] Days of operating cash plus enough cash and liquid marketable securities to cover current liabilities and donor-restricted net assets.

If your ministry has significant debt, it may be appropriate to display metrics such as debt service reserves (in months) or debt payments as a percentage of year-to-date revenue.

2. Program and Impact

	Target	6 months ago	Now
Complete the program metrics segments based on your most significant programs.			

3. Human Resources

	Target	6 months ago	Now
Staff turnover in last year	3%	5%	10%
Open unemployment compensation claims	Not more than 3	5	4

It is often difficult to communicate a summary of human resources-related data. This is why human resources data is usually not communicated to the board at all.

4. Board of Directors

	Target	6 months ago	Now
Attendance at board meetings	95%	75%	85%
Annual CEO performance evaluation completed on time	By February 15	Not applicable	Done by February 10
Pool of new board member prospects	10	8	6

5. Fundraising

	Target	6 months ago	Now
Lapsed donors in last 6 months	200	175	220
New Individual donors in last 6 months	300	200	410

6. Compliance and Risk Management

	Target	6 months ago	Now
Form 990 and 990-T filed on time	By November 15	Not applicable	Applied for extension on 10-25
Annual filings with applicate states to maintain corporate status	By July 31	Not applicable	Filed July 30

Summary. It is hard to imagine driving your car without quick, easy access to a speedometer, fuel guage, or gear position. Without an effective dashboard, a ministry lacks a fast way to check on the basics so you can spend less time on where you have been and more time on where you are going.

BOARDROOM LESSON

The hard work in communicating data isn't in
producing and sharing a vast quantity of it;
it is in selecting the right information to communicate
and then determining how to make the data tell the story.

Board Action Steps:

○ 1. **Agree:** As part of the accountability process, the board
chair and the CEO should agree on what data will be
visually presented through dashboards.

○ 2. **Communicate:** Highlight the selected elements that
tell an interesting dashboard story.

○ 3. **Improve:** Review dashboards periodically to determine
how to improve their effectiveness.

Prayer
Lord, we don't want to splatter the walls
with unending and overwhelming charts and graphs.
Help us simplify our dashboard reporting techniques
to enhance our governance.
Amen.

6 ENHANCE HARMONY BY CLARIFYING YOUR PARTICIPANT-HAT EXPECTATIONS

Understand the three board hats:
Governance, Volunteer, and Participant.

The best boards communicate their Participant-Hat expectations
to current and new board members with a simple tool,
The Board Member Annual Affirmation Statement.[1]

ECFA Governance Toolbox Series No. 2: Balancing Board Roles

There's a familiar scene, almost as common as Bill Murray's character in *Groundhog Day*, played out in boardrooms across the country.

CEO: We had a tremendous event last Saturday at the center. I know you're all busy, but many of our volunteers asked why our board members didn't participate. I do want to thank Carolyn for coming, so at least the board was represented by one member.

Translation: I'm really ticked off that board members aren't highly committed to this ministry. *Don't you care about our clients?* Our staff and volunteers are constantly wondering—*out loud*—why you're even on the board. I'm so disappointed, and I can't keep covering for your lack of participation in these important events.

It doesn't have to be this way. Unspoken expectations will also poison the culture—the heart and soul—of a board. But first, how would you define reality in your boardroom? Which scenario describes your board's experience?

Scenario 1: Hinting. A week before the work day or walk-a-thon, your CEO or board chair hints that it would be helpful if board members participated.

Scenario 2: Whining. After the work day or walk-a-thon, your CEO or board chair whines that it would have been helpful if more board members had participated.

Scenario 3: Affirming. At the beginning of each year, a simple tool, The Board Member Annual Affirmation Statement,[2] lists the Participant-Hat "attendance-required events." All board members affirm their high commitment to participate or ask to be excused.

Affirming is certainly favored over hinting and whining. For example, new board members should know—up front—if hosting a table of 10 at the fundraising dinner is a required Participant Hat event. Glossing over their lack of advance planning, some CEOs and/or staff members often default to clever guilt tactics to prod board members into showing up. That's inappropriate and unfair—and hardly God-honoring!

The solution is simple. The best boards customize their own Board Member Annual Affirmation Statement by communicating board member roles and responsibilities with three hats:

- The **Governance Hat** section delineates governance roles and responsibilities, along with an annual calendar of board and committee meeting dates, the annual (or every-other-year) board retreat, and other governance-related calendar items.

- The **Volunteer Hat** section clarifies the protocol for how board members may serve as volunteers and spells out the appropriate reporting relationships. It also notes why board members should not wear their Governance Hats when volunteering.

- The **Participant Hat** section describes the special events (including fundraising events, as detailed in board policies) that board members, and perhaps spouses, are expected to attend—again without their Governance Hats.

> *The Participant-Hat section describes the special events (including fundraising events, as detailed in board policies) that board members, and perhaps spouses, are expected to attend.*

Why is this so important? There are at least five stakeholder segments that must understand the three hats. And good news—The Board Member Annual Affirmation Statement tool will help bring clarity to each important group!

1. **Board members** will be informed up front of the organization's realistic expectations regarding attendance at ministry events. This annual affirmation also adds rich meaning to the spiritual calling of board service and inspires high commitment.

2. **The CEO and the board** will be singing from the same song sheet.

3. **Spouses of board members** will review the annual affirmation statement each year and note Participant Hat commitments for the family calendar.

4. **Senior team members and all staff** will have a common lexicon—the three hats—and will not hint or whine about board member engagement expectations that have not been agreed upon in advance.

5. **Volunteers** (often a source of board prospects) will be educated about the appropriate role of the board and the organization's commitment to leverage the strengths, spiritual gifts, and passion of each person. (Some board members, after all, should not be trusted with a hammer, saw, or paint brush on the annual work day if they are not gifted with those tools!)

Guilt and shaming are a poor substitute for clarity and inspiration. Think back to your last board meeting when there was a Participant Hat discussion. Did your board chair's comments or your CEO's body language communicate healthy, God-honoring governance? Or did the veiled expectations need a translation?

Your board members, similar to your volunteers, will respond when you appeal to high ideals, not mixed messages. Al Newell, the founder and CEO of High Impact Volunteer Ministry Development, says that if you pursue discipleship, motivation will follow:

> Sustaining motivation is better understood as a by-product as opposed to a goal of itself. It is my experience that if you pursue discipleship with volunteers [and board members], motivation will

follow. If volunteers see the fulfillment of their role as "obeying and serving God" rather than serving you or your organization, it will cause motivation to swell.[3]

BOARDROOM LESSON

Stop hinting and whining about board member attendance at organizational events. Instead, include all attendance expectations and dates in a simple tool, The Board Member Annual Affirmation Statement.

Board Action Steps:

○ **1. View and Engage:** Leverage the *ECFA Governance Toolbox Series No. 2: Balancing Board Roles.*

○ **2. Create:** Download "The Board Member Annual Affirmation Statement" (see the tools and templates in the *ECFA Governance Toolbox Series No. 2)* and customize it for your board.

○ **3. Order:** Purchase *ECFA Tools and Templates for Effective Board Governance: Time-Saving Solutions for Your Board* by Dan Busby and John Pearson and download 22 templates, including the "Board Member Annual Affirmation Statement."[4]

Prayer
Lord, forgive us for hinting and whining and
communicating unhealthy, mixed messages
about attendance at ministry events.
Help us instead to communicate with clarity.
Amen.

7 | ELIMINATE FUZZINESS BETWEEN BOARD AND STAFF ROLES

Keep your leaders on track with a one-page *Prime Responsibility Chart.*

> *The difference between micromanaging and appropriate questioning is not always a bright line. What really defines micromanaging is not whether a board member is digging into details. It's really a question of which details and for what purpose.*[1]
>
> Ram Charan

Picture this. In the middle of a routine board meeting, the amiable board chair had reached his limit. Two board members were aggressively and inappropriately arguing (actually, they were shouting) over a very inconsequential issue—not even an agenda topic.

Rap! Rap! Rap! Rap! Rap! Shockingly, the board chair gaveled the boisterous board members into an embarrassing state of silence. The room went deathly quiet and this Christ-centered board (*at least the core values said the board aspired to be "Christ-centered"*) faced a common boardroom dilemma: the fuzziness between board and staff roles.

These two outspoken board members profoundly (*profoundly!*) disagreed on whether the topic was a board issue or a staff issue.

Sound familiar? In our experience, these mini-battles (and major wars) are fought routinely in boardrooms worldwide. Here are just a few examples:

- A fundraising letter aggressively requests an immediate response at a time when the ministry has 12 months of cash reserves in the bank. *Staff issue or board issue?*

- The ministry has used a significant portion of their restricted net assets for operating expenses. *Staff issue or board issue?*

- A board member suggests that annual updates of the staff handbook should be reviewed by the full board. *Staff issue or board issue?*

- While the board annually evaluates the CEO's performance, apparently the CEO does not conduct formal performance reviews of her direct reports. *Staff issue or board issue?*

- A vice president appears to be overly generous in granting bonuses, days off, and other perks to hard-working people in his department. Other VPs are complaining to the CEO and the board. *Staff issue or board issue?*

We could go on and on—but you get the idea. You likely have more examples from recent board meetings, and you would not be alone. ECFA research found that the biggest contrast between effective and ineffective boards is the issue of role clarity. In a survey of ECFA board members, we asked if they agreed that "our board understands its roles and responsibilities." Among effective boards, 93 percent did. Among ineffective boards, only 44 percent did. That's a 49 percent difference![2]

So what's the role of the board?

- ❑ **Ministering?** Listening, encouraging, praying with department heads?

- ❑ **Monitoring?** Ensuring that every department has goals, reports, and results?

- ❑ **Meddling?** Jumping in with new ideas, fixing problems, addressing personnel issues?

- ❑ **Micro-managing?** In the weeds, obsessing over details, mandating lengthy reports?

Our recommendation is that most boards should relate to one employee: the CEO. When decisions involve the CEO with his or her direct reports, those should be delegated to the CEO, but the CEO should not violate any board-approved policies. There are many tools that will help clarify these relationships, such as a Board Policies Manual (see Lesson 4 in *Lessons From the Nonprofit Boardroom*[3]).

These two outspoken board members profoundly (profoundly!) disagreed on whether the topic was a board issue or a staff issue.

Try this tool: the *Prime Responsibility Chart* (PRC) shown on page 43. The PRC will help you eliminate fuzziness between board and staff roles. The PRC is short—just one page. Roles and responsibilities are crystal clear. Based on your ministry's governance model, you may have a unique approach to some functions, but you can customize the PRC to meet your needs.

Our recommendation is that boards should relate to one employee: the CEO.

Prime Responsibility Chart[4]
Version 3.0 (Updated on January 15, 20XX)

Important! This template is an example only.
It is not prescriptive for every ministry.

P =Prime Responsibility	A = Assistant Responsibility	AP = Approval Required		

ROLES AND RESPONSIBILITIES FOR BOARD AND STAFF	Board	CEO	CFO or COO	Department Heads
PERSONNEL				
1) Hire and fire the CEO	P			
2) Hire and fire other senior leaders		P		
3) Hire and fire department heads		AP	P	
4) Hire and fire staff		AP	AP	P
5) Annual update: employee handbook	AP	AP	P	A
MINISTRY PLANNING				
1) Mission, vision, values	AP	P	A	A
2) Rolling 3-year Ministry Plan Annual Update	AP	A	P	A
3) CEO annual goals	AP	P	A	A
4) Department heads' annual goals		AP	AP	P
FINANCE				
1) Annual budget	AP	A	P	A
2) Quarterly financial reports			P	
3) Annual audit	AP		P	
4) Non-budgeted expenditures over $_____		AP	P	A
Add additional categories, roles, and responsibilities below (as needed)				

Update this chart whenever the board edits the policy and also update the version (example): Version 4.0—April 15, 20XX

The chart is simple and straightforward and can be changed at any time—literally at any or every meeting. Growth (or decline) in your organization or a department will likely impact reporting relationships, so this tool is not static—it's meant to be reviewed frequently. When the PRC is edited by board action, just make the change and update the chart with "Version 4.0" and the current date, and then email the revised PRC to board members and department heads within 24 hours. Also, have copies available for reference at every board meeting.

The most important principle: only one person has "Prime Responsibility" (P). This one-page chart is an excellent way to clarify board and staff roles.

We close with this reminder: a PRC will not solve all of your staff/board issues. Pray, discern, and inspire your board to a high-level of courtesy and thoughtful discussion. We appreciate Ram Charan's insightful chapter, "How Do We Stop From Micromanaging?" in his book, *Owning Up: The 14 Questions Every Board Member Needs to Ask*. He writes:

> "Asking questions of an operating nature is not in itself micromanaging, as long as the questions lead to insights about issues like strategy, performance, major investment decisions, key personnel, the choice of goals, or risk assessment."[5]

And did we mention how our CEO friend resolved the ***Rap! Rap! Rap! Rap! Rap!*** drama at future board meetings?

"No problem," our colleague told us. "Amazingly, the chairman's gavel mysteriously disappeared—and was never seen again."

BOARDROOM LESSON

Clarify board and staff roles with the one-page
Prime Responsibility Chart. The PRC is a helpful tool
to eliminate current and future fuzziness
on roles and responsibilities.

Board Action Steps:

○ **1. Clarify:** Is your board/CEO/staff organizational chart crystal clear?

○ **2. Create:** Customize Version 3.0 of the *Prime Responsibility Chart* and present it at your next board meeting for both board and staff feedback. Then edit and produce Version 4.0.[6]

○ **3. Congratulate:** At the end of any lengthy discussion at a board meeting, affirm and congratulate (maybe with a Chick-fil-A gift card) the first board member who observes: "This is taking way too long to decide. Is it because we need to add or edit a line on our *Prime Responsibility Chart?*"

Prayer
Lord, enable our board to focus on governance
agenda items, and to stay out of the weeds—
so our board meetings don't become staff meetings.
Amen.

8 | DESIGN YOUR SUCCESSION PLAN— NOW!

What if your CEO is hit by a bus?

*One of the toughest things any leader can do is hand off
the baton of leadership to another leader of the organization.
It takes planning and forethought . . .
it's necessary for outgoing leaders to keep their egos in check
while letting go of one of the things they love most.*[1]

John C. Maxwell

Here's a practical tool—with a memorable exercise—that your board will never, ever forget!

Ask a board member, a senior team member, or a consultant to facilitate a 15-minute exercise at your next board meeting. We call it the "What if our CEO is hit by a bus?" exercise. If your CEO or your board members are reluctant to talk about succession planning—this poignant drill (and video) will get your succession juices flowing! (See the last page of this lesson for more details.)

Why is this important? William Vanderbloemen and Warren Bird note, "Everyone wants to talk about succession . . . until it's their own."[2] Indeed, ECFA research found that fewer than one in three boards have a written CEO succession plan. Only 31 percent said yes to, "Does your board have a written succession plan in the event of your CEO's death, long-term illness or unexpected resignation?"[3]

Every CEO is an interim CEO. Even founders die! So boards have two options: plan for succession—or be unprepared for succession. We recommend planning—because the stakes are high! Your board's decision-making and discernment process will have eternal consequences.

The board's selection of the CEO, says David McKenna, "separates Christ-centered organizations from other organizations because it is a sacred trust." McKenna

Every CEO is an interim CEO.

adds, "Like the ripple effect of a stone tossed into a pond, the CEO's influence will move in waves through generations. No decision of the board, absolutely no decision, is more profound."[4]

We encourage boards—even boards with new CEOs—to use the helpful tools and resources in the *ECFA Governance Toolbox Series No. 4: Succession Planning—Eleven Principles for Successful Successions: "Every CEO Is an Interim CEO."*[5]

What if…

. . . your CEO is hit by a bus and dies?

. . . your CEO is incapacitated?

. . . your CEO has lost all passion for the ministry—and knows it?

. . . your CEO has lost all passion—and doesn't know it or won't admit it?

This *ECFA Governance Toolbox Series* can be your catalyst for addressing succession planning—and moving the muted conversations from the hallways and onto your board's agenda. The boardroom—where you can leverage prayer, spiritual discernment, and the wisdom of many counselors— is the perfect place to address this elephant in the room.

Here's a brief summary of the 11 succession planning principles—a "101 course" in understanding the important difference between executive transition and succession planning.

Principle 1 – Avoid buses and boredom!

Peter Drucker famously said, "Fortunately or unfortunately, the one predictable thing in any organization is the crisis."[6] Effective boards are not fearful of the future—they are faithful in addressing both emergency succession issues and long-term succession planning. Effective boards pray for protection yet establish appropriate policy—and thus are prepared for a future crisis.

Principle 2 – Discern your board's succession values and beliefs

Before your board's CEO succession planning discussion spirals into the nuts and bolts, stop the presses! Take time to review your organization's mission, vision and core values. Then discern: what are our deeply held beliefs about leadership, spiritual discernment, and succession planning?

True or False? "Appointment without anointment always leads to disaster."

"I know of few Christian leaders today who were anointed before they were appointed," writes R. Scott Rodin. "We have mostly employed the business model of doing careful searches, looking for Christian leaders who we can appoint to office.

We check their credentials, put them through rigorous interviews and give them psychological tests before we make the critical appointment. Once they are in place, we then anoint them and ask God to bless their work."

Rodin adds, "The biblical evidence seems to indicate that God selects leaders in the opposite order. Samuel anointed David before appointing him king. The selection criterion for leadership was not based on who seemed most fit for the appointment, but on whom God had anointed for the task. And appointment without anointment always led to disaster."[7]

Principle 3 – Inspire your CEO to thrive with a God-honoring lifestyle

Is your CEO thriving or just surviving? An effective succession planning process begins by ensuring that your board invests time (and accountability) in CEO soul care (see Lesson 4). When your CEO lives and models a God-honoring and healthy lifestyle, he or she will likely serve your ministry longer with greater faithfulness and fruitfulness. And potential internal candidates will already affirm and practice this core value.

In *NEXT: Pastoral Succession That Works*, William Vanderbloemen and Warren Bird recommend that boards create sabbatical policies, mandate vacations and days off, and inspire leaders to be in accountability groups. After examining almost 200 pastoral succession case studies, they conclude, "Too many successions are on the heels of a moral or financial failure. And nearly every one of those failures happened because the [leaders] were tired and didn't have anyone to talk to about their personal fatigue."[8]

Principle 4 – Model successful succession in the boardroom first

Read this next line, in unison, at your next board meeting:

> "There are no dysfunctional organizations—
> only dysfunctional boards."

Then add:

> "There are no dysfunctional succession plans—
> only dysfunctional boards that allow mediocre planning
> to occur."

Boards are better equipped to address CEO succession if they have already been faithful in planning for the ongoing succession of board chairs and board members who retire, cycle off, or otherwise need to be replaced on the board.

Principle 5 – Delegate succession planning to the appropriate committee

There is a substantial difference between executive transition and succession planning. According to Nancy Axelrod, "The search for a new chief executive is an intermittent event that is timeline-driven. Succession planning, on the other hand, reflects an ongoing, continuous process that boards (with the help of their chief executive) implement."[9]

Succession planning should be assigned to the committee or task force that fits your board culture. This may be an executive committee, a governance or nominating committee, or a succession planning task force if there is no current plan in place. Give the committee two tasks:

1. Preparing for an emergency transition

2. Creating a long-term succession planning mindset and culture throughout the organization

Principle 6 – Invest in growing your leaders (every leader needs a coach)

Some board members might push back: "What happens if we invest in developing our people and then they leave us?" But the better question is: "What happens if we don't, and they stay?"

The ongoing process of succession planning will be smoother (and often seamless) when your board invests in the professional growth of your current CEO. When your top leader is a lifelong learner and open to feedback, he or she will inspire the entire team to grow. Bill Conaty and Ram Charan set this high bar beautifully:

What happens if we invest in developing our people and then they leave us? But the better question is: What happens if we don't, and they stay?

> Only one competency lasts.
> It is the ability to create a steady, self-renewing
> stream of leaders.[10]

Principle 7 – Trust God and discern direction

Boards that are blessed with God-honoring men and women will have a culture of spiritually discerning God's voice in every board meeting. Don't wait until the eleventh hour of a succession planning crisis to get on your knees. Practice spiritual discernment early and often! Consider this caution from Ruth Haley Barton: "It is also important to involve the right people. One very common leadership mistake is to think that we can take a group of undiscerning individuals and expect them to show up in a leadership setting and all of a sudden become discerning!"[11]

Principles 8, 9, and 10 – Planning for Plans A, B, and C

Address the elephant in the room! Your CEO will retire or accept another assignment someday, as will the senior leaders reporting to the CEO. Healthy boards and healthy CEOs address these facts of life—with prayer, discernment, and transparent conversations. The toolbox materials will help you create plans for three scenarios:

- **Plan A – Your CEO retires.** Does the organization have board-approved policies to address CEO succession? Could the CEO's retirement occur in the next five years? Has the CEO begun to plan for retirement by finding a "retirement mentor"—a wise confidant who has "ended well" and has permission to speak truth into the CEO's situation?

- **Plan B – Your CEO resigns.** Does the board have a signed "Memo of Understanding" (or contract) between the board and the CEO that requires advance notice of X weeks (or months) upon submitting a letter of resignation? Is the board prepared to quickly and effectively put "next steps" in place when a letter of resignation is submitted? What is the board's protocol for appointing an interim CEO?

- **Plan C – Your CEO is terminated.** Donald Rumsfeld advises, "Never hire anyone you can't fire."[12] So did your board have frank discussions with your current CEO regarding the when/if scenarios that would prompt a termination?

Is your board prepared to spot potential problems early on, or will the board wait to address issues only "when all else fails?" If the board faces a situation where the CEO must be terminated, are board members adequately prepared to exit the CEO in a God-honoring and appropriately confidential way?

Principle 11 – Discern if a search firm would be helpful

The toolbox materials list three options that a board might consider when searching for a new CEO: retaining a search firm, retaining a consultant/coach, or conducting your own search. And note this wisdom: select the option based on your mission and vision—not today's budget.

Finally, heed this insight from Michael J. Lotito: "If you spend a lot of time figuring out who you're going to hire, you'll have to spend far less time figuring out who to fire."[13]

Ram Charan reminds boards: "There is nothing more important for a CEO than having the right strategy and right choice of goals, and for the board, the right strategy is second only to having the right CEO."[14] When your CEO exits (whether for Plan A, B, or C), it's time for board members to execute their fiduciary and spiritual duty. No one, except the board, has this God-given stewardship responsibility.

BOARDROOM LESSON

If your CEO were to be hit by a bus today—
is your board prepared for the executive transition?
Your current CEO will one day be your former CEO.
Christ-centered boards address succession planning—
not with fear—but with faith,
believing that God will lead them.

Board Action Steps:

○ **1. Design:** Facilitate a "What if our CEO is hit by a bus?" 15-minute exercise for your next board meeting. Download the "Facilitator Guide" from the *ECFA Governance Toolbox Series No. 4: Succession Planning— Eleven Principles for Successful Successions.*[15] (Visit *www.ECFA.org/toolbox.*) Follow the four steps and screen the short video, "The Bus Ride to Eternity."

○ **2. Delegate:** Appoint a committee or task force to address executive transition and long-term succession planning. Study biblical examples of leadership succession, including Moses and Joshua, David and Solomon, Elijah and Elisha, and Paul and Timothy. Put the plan in writing and ensure that your Board Policies Manual addresses succession policies.

Prayer
Lord, You've told us in 1 Thessalonians 5:24 (NIV)
that 'the One who calls you is faithful and
He will do it.' So we rest in this assurance
as we discern Your will during our next
executive transition—according to Your timing.
Amen.

PART 3:

NOMINEES FOR THE
BOARD MEMBER HALL OF FAME

Boards really can add value to the organizations they serve. Board members really can work together in meaningful and rewarding ways. And even though we all have imperfections, governance excellence really is possible.[1]

Patrick Lencioni

9 | JUST DO ONE THING A MONTH

Make a specific ask of each board member each month.

When we clarified the opportunities for board member participation between board meetings, we celebrated the highest board member engagement we had ever experienced!

One Happy Board Chair

Board members often grimace and admit to me, "I don't think I'm doing enough as a board member, but I'm not sure how I can be of more help. I don't want to micromanage or assume a staff position. I just wish there was more clarity about the expectations of my role on the board in between meetings."

Good news! A board member recently shared a brilliant solution to this dilemma—thus his nomination to the Board Member Hall of Fame!

I was consulting with a ministry board at its annual weekend retreat. A new board member made a presentation based on his expertise in his day job—he's the senior vice president of advancement for a major state university. In addition to sharing the latest trends in giving, what motivates givers, and how to grow giving, he shared this insight with his new board colleagues.

Every month he contacts the institution's board of directors and reminds them:

**"Just do one thing a month
for our university!"**

This innovative leader provided the board members with a grocery list of ways they can inspire, influence, and impact other people for the university's important mission.

Your ministry's list of "Just Do One Thing" will be unique to your cause, but it might include these ideas:

Just Do One Thing a Month:

- ❑ Set up a lunch meeting with a prospective giver and your CEO.

- ❑ Invite a colleague to a ministry event.

- ❑ Open a door at a family foundation.

- ❑ Host a prayer gathering for the ministry.

- ❑ Pray, then send a sacrificial gift.

- ❑ Call current major givers to say thanks for their faithfulness.

- ❑ Other: _____

Imagine the clarity and confidence you'll create when your board members know that if they do just one thing a month for your ministry, they will have a sense of "I'm being faithful."

And speaking of clarity, be sure to distinguish between the board member's three hats (Governance, Volunteer, Participant) when establishing "Just Do One Thing a Month" expectations.

To enlighten your board regarding the three hats, view the short video in the *ECFA Governance Toolbox Series No. 2: Balancing Board Roles.*[1] (See also Lessons 6 and 7.)

Imagine the clarity and confidence you'll create when your board members know that if they do just one thing a month for your ministry, they will have a sense of "I'm being faithful."

For your ministry, perhaps the communication comes from the CEO, and the opportunities for the month include a broader range of topics, including a specific prayer list.

Matthew 25:23 reads, "The master said, 'Well done, my good and faithful servant. You have been faithful in handling this small amount, so now I will give you many more responsibilities. Let's celebrate together!'" (NLT)

BOARDROOM LESSON

Board members should be appropriately involved with your ministry. Providing specific opportunities for engagement each month is a key to meaningful involvement.

Board Action Steps:

○ **1. Create:** Develop your grocery list of "Just Do One Thing a Month" ideas for the ministry.

○ **2. Communicate:** Call or email the board members individually each month and ask, "Have you done your 'One Thing' this month?"

○ **3. Celebrate:** At each board meeting, highlight what has been achieved through the "One Thing" initiative and celebrate God's blessings on the ministry.

Prayer

Lord, we ask Your blessing on this One Thing a Month opportunity—not as a gimmick, but as a Kingdom initiative that will challenge our board members to meaningful involvement.
Amen.

10 | A UNANIMOUS CHOICE FOR THE BOARD MEMBER HALL OF FAME

She limits her service to one board at a time.

The Law of Diminishing Board Impact:
The more boards on which an individual serves,
the less impact that individual will have on each board.

Why should someone be a shoo-in for the Board Member Hall of Fame? There are many reasons, but the one overriding reason is that she limits her service on boards to *one board at a time.*

Is it possible for an individual to provide quality board service on multiple boards at the same time? In some rare instances, it may be. However, serving on multiple boards generally causes the Law of Diminishing Board Impact to kick in. It can leave you saying, "In our desire to have high-profile individuals join our board, we had buyer's remorse because we ignored the impact of the multiple boards on which they were already serving."

By choosing to serve on only one board at a time, she can:

We had buyer's remorse because we ignored the impact of the multiple boards on which they were already serving.

- **Focus on praying for the ministry.** What ministry leader wouldn't want a board member focusing on prayer for their ministry?

- **Call the CEO, send the CEO encouraging emails, and respond to emails from the CEO in a timely manner.** Being the CEO of a ministry can be very lonely. There are few people with whom CEOs can talk at a deep level. Receiving an encouraging call or email from a board member means so much to CEOs. When the CEO sends an update to board members, it is so encouraging to the CEO to receive a timely response from each board member—even a brief response saying "With you."

> *In our desire to have high-profile individuals join our board, we had buyer's remorse because we ignored the impact of the multiple boards on which they were already serving.*

- **Attend all board and committee meetings.** Serving on more than one board at a time increases the possibility of missing meetings for one of the boards because of conflicting dates.

- **Be available for volunteering.** Serving on only one board helps ensure she will have time to volunteer for the ministry.

- **Implement unconflicted opportunities to raise funds for the ministry.** Board members often raise funds for the ministry they represent. When individuals serve on multiple boards, it may be very challenging (perhaps impossible) to appropriately prioritize competing appeals when inviting friends and colleagues to give to one or more ministries.

- **Increase the possibility of joyful service.** Serving on one board at a time increases the possibility of achieving joy through board service and dramatically decreases the time pressure that often robs board members of true joy.

- **Include the ministry in her giving.** Serving on one board allows her to include the ministry in her giving—hopefully making the ministry one of her top three priorities in terms of annual giving.

Ultimately, serving as a board member for multiple ministries at the same time may be appropriate for a few individuals, but from a ministry perspective, serving on one board at a time is the ideal.

BOARDROOM LESSON

The qualifications for hall-of-fame board members are not based simply on impressive resumés or years of board service. We honor people who passionately commit abundant time and energy to serve on one board at a time. Combined with God-honoring competencies and humility, that will always outweigh mere credentials and years of service.

Board Action Steps:

○ 1. **Inquire:** When "dating" a board prospect (see Lesson 18), ask about current involvement on other boards and assess the length of those commitments.

○ 2. **Include:** When determining if a board prospect has adequate time for board service, include all of that person's additional responsibilities (work, family, church, etc.) in your evaluation.

○ 3. **Inspire:** Set the bar high for your Board Prospect Pipeline and inspire your board to add only the names of people who would resonate with the "one board at a time" core value.

Prayer

Lord, guide us to prospects who will affirm board service as a sacred calling and will prioritize their time, talent, and treasure for Kingdom purposes.
Amen.

11 | THRIVE WITH FOUR KINGDOM VALUES

Set a high standard for the board and the board members.

The place God calls you to is the place where your deep gladness and the world's deep hunger meet.[1]

Frederick Buechner

A CEO friend, Chuck, once told me, "I don't have the spiritual gift of board meetings." He expressed what many ministry leaders feel.

Too often, board members do not thrive at board meetings because one or more of these dysfunctions are present:

- Board members with inadequate training for their board responsibilities

- Board members with gifts ill-suited for the primary role of governance

- Board members with fuzzy understanding of board/staff roles

- Board members with personal agendas—and an inability to discern God's agenda

- Board members with limited theological acumen

- Board members with unhealthy character issues and insufficient grace

No board is perfect, but the best boards set a high standard for board service. When the right people—with the right motives and God-honoring character—serve graciously together, there will be a minimum amount of dysfunction and a maximum amount of spiritual fruit and impact. Board members and CEOs will *thrive* in board meetings as the Holy Spirit deploys their spiritual gifts and their God-designed personalities and strengths.

So what would that look like in your boardroom? We believe that a nominee to the Board Member Hall of Fame would demonstrate these Kingdom values:

1. **DISCERNMENT:** Calling and Passion. Look around your board table. Would every person affirm that God has called them to board service? John Pellowe writes, "The Holy Spirit can nudge us towards those good works that God has prepared for us to do (Ephesians 2:10); this nudging is usually described as a call." He adds, "God's individual call is normally in line with the gifts that you already have."[2]

    Pellowe also cautions those who consider ministry and board service—that if the "mission is not closely tied to your interests, your board service will be a draining experience..."[3]

    Steve Macchia believes that "Passion is the fuel that keeps the engine of your vision alive." He suggests you answer this fill-in-the-blank question: "What energizes me the most is my passionate concern for _____."[4] *Is board service and the mission of the ministry extremely high on your passion list—or did you agree to serve without regard to calling and passion?*

Boards must be highly competent in spiritually discerning God's voice—as individuals and as a board. Who should serve on the board? Who should chair the board? What is God's agenda? According to David McKenna, "Discernment is a gift of the Holy Spirit that comes with spiritual maturity. It may well be the gift that defines Christ-centered leadership."[5]

2. **DEPLOYMENT:** Spiritual Gifts. The reason Chuck said he didn't have the spiritual gift of board meetings is because he didn't! (*We know. We know. "Attending board meetings" is not a spiritual gift—but keep reading.*) Frankly, Chuck was not cut out to be a leader—and he was savvy enough to recognize it.

Not everyone is gifted to serve in leadership as a board member. According to Romans 12, 1 Corinthians 12, and Ephesians 4 (and elsewhere), God has given every believer one or more spiritual gifts. Paul encouraged Timothy, "Do not neglect the spiritual gift within you" (1 Timothy 4:14 NASB).

Thriving boards are astute at deploying the spiritual gifts around the board table—and discerning what gifts are needed. The best boards inspire members to leverage their God-given gifts. The best boards don't just fill board slots by inserting square pegs in round holes.

While we recommend that the CEO not serve as board chair—for many reasons—one reason is that the CEO is sometimes not spiritually gifted or temperamentally equipped to serve as the chair. If the CEO is also the board chair, he or she is often placed squarely in the middle of challenging, and sometimes contentious, debates. For a serious gut check on the crucial role of board chair, read David McKenna's powerful book—just 119 pages—*Call of the Chair: Leading the Board of the Christ-centered Ministry.*[6]

3. **COMMITMENT:** Faithful and Fruitful. Throughout this book you'll read dozens of board best practices and expectations. It may be overwhelming to the first-time board member. But don't quit! 1 Thessalonians 5:24 says, "The one who calls you is faithful, and he will do it" (NIV).

> *The best boards inspire members to leverage their God-given gifts. The best boards don't just fill board slots by inserting square pegs in round holes.*

Ensure that the position description and expectations for board members are in writing—and reviewed at least annually. As we suggest in Lesson 6, use a *Board Member Annual Affirmation Statement* and create a holy moment for the board at the first board meeting of the year. Connect the dots between faithfulness and fruitfulness—and review God's blessing on the ministry over the past year, at least in part, because of the faithfulness and diligence of your board.

4. **ENJOYMENT: Experience God's Pleasure.** Board service can be immensely enjoyable. *Honest!* Our friend and colleague, Mike Pate, reminds us frequently that his favorite day of the month is the day there is a board meeting.

When board members leverage their spiritual gifts,[7] their strengths (see the *Discover Your CliftonStrengths* assessment[8]), and their God-given social styles (analytical, driving, amiable, or expressive),[9] they experience extraordinary fulfillment and joy. That's God's plan for us! If board service feels draining and debilitating for you, then consider another area of service "where your deep gladness and the world's deep hunger meet," as Frederick Buechner so aptly put it.[10]

"When I run, I feel His pleasure," said Eric Liddell in *Chariots of Fire.*[11] Imagine if on the way home from your board meeting, every (*every!*) board member exclaimed, "When I engage in the board's holy work—I feel God's pleasure!"

Discernment, deployment, commitment, and enjoyment— reflect on these four Kingdom values as you inspire people to serve on your board. Those are Board Member Hall of Fame values.

BOARDROOM LESSON

Invite people to serve on your board who have
high passion for your mission and ministry—and who
discern board service as a holy calling. Inspire board
members to leverage their spiritual gifts and strengths—
or their experience will be draining and joyless.

Board Action Steps:

○ **1. Discern:** What Kingdom values are foundational to
your board's theology and philosophy of governance?

○ **2. Deploy:** Provide board members with assessment
resources to identify spiritual gifts, strengths, and social
styles—and then leverage the unique giftedness of each
board member.[12]

○ **3. Declare:** Raise the bar—and create the expectation that
all board members will experience God's pleasure as
they serve.

Prayer

Lord, like Eric Liddell's testimony, *"I believe
that God made me for a purpose, but He also
made me fast,"*[13] show each of our board members
their God-given purpose.
Amen.

12 | KEEPING THE BOARDROOM AFLOAT

Are too many staff causing the
boardroom to capsize?

*At my first board meeting, I remember not being able
to distinguish board members from senior staff.*[1]

Robert C. Andringa and Ted W. Engstrom

What is the right number of staff to attend nonprofit board meetings? This question is not on the radar of most boards. The median board size of ECFA nonprofit members is 10 members, with one of them being a paid staff member. However, there are many extreme examples such as the board with 40 total members, 15 of whom are paid staff.[2]

Until a balcony is required in the boardroom to accommodate non-voting staff members, the danger of a staff takeover of the governing process may not be evident.

Nonprofit boards need input from staff members. Most CEOs do not feel adequate to report on behalf of all other staff members. So, how does a board get staff input without the boardroom becoming overpopulated by ministry staff?

For openers, let's get this question out of the way: Is it possible for the boardroom to capsize? The answer is unequivocally yes. You may think you have not experienced it. In fact, it may be happening in your organization right now and no one recognizes that boardroom imbalance has occurred.

Perhaps the CEO is the only staff person who attends your board meetings. If so, capsizing the boardroom is not a concern.

But at what point does the boardroom capsize? Is there a magic maximum number of staff in the boardroom? Is there a percentage limit of staff members to board members? There is no red line, magic number, or litmus test.

Some boards hit stormy seas when only one non-voting staff member other than the CEO is in the room, but capsizing usually requires more than one. Finding the balance requires discretion, wisdom, perception, and seasoned boardroom experience.

There are practical ways to avoid staff capsizing the boardroom:

Determining the best number of non-voting staff in the boardroom requires discretion, wisdom, perception, and seasoned boardroom experience.

- **Staff do not attend the meeting—submitting only written reports.** Using this approach, only the CEO attends board meetings. Other staff members routinely submit their written reports. The CEO responds to any questions raised by the board concerning staff reports.

- **Staff attend the meeting to report and then depart.** In this scenario, the CEO is the only staff member who attends the entire board meeting. Individual staff members are present only when and if they present reports to the board.

A good barometer for whether the staff members are causing too many waves in the boardroom is to observe the dynamic that is created by their presence. Here are a few points of possible sensitivity to watch for when including non-voting staff members other than the CEO:

- **Is the presence of non-voting staff members in the boardroom conducive to good board governance?** If a staff member's presence in the boardroom does not enhance the governance process, it is easy to make the case that the staff member should not be present.

- **Do non-voting staff members interject comments into a board session without being called upon for their input?** When a staff member feels free to interject unsolicited comments, this is an indication that the staff person is functioning more like a board member than a staff member.

- **Do non-voting staff members take a position in opposition to the stance of the CEO?** If one or more staff members are not in agreement with the position of the CEO on a certain matter, objections should be discussed before the board meeting. Then the staff member needs to follow the CEO's recommendation. Otherwise, the staff member does not belong in the boardroom—period.

  Wise CEOs will solicit contrarian views in staff meetings so there is staff agreement in board meetings.

  It is incumbent, however, on the CEO to brief staff before the board meeting—so everyone is on the same page. Wise CEOs will solicit contrarian views in staff meetings so there is staff agreement in board meetings.

- **Do non-voting staff members use nonverbal communication to indicate their approval or disapproval of comments made by board members?** It may be a furtive glance, a frown, or a smile that immediately sends a message of where the staff member stands on the issue. While nonverbal messaging might be ignored by board members, this communication could impact the vote of one or more board members and change the outcome of an important decision.

- **Do board members ask questions of non-voting staff, not intending to seek more information but giving the staff member an opportunity to "make a speech" that aligns with the position of the board member?** Boardroom etiquette tip: When board members have questions, they could direct them to the board chair or to the CEO and let them decide whether to ask for input from a non-voting staff member. When board members begin to address questions directly to staff, the CEO's position may be inappropriately diminished.

If the answer to any of the above questions is yes, then you may be entering turbulent waters and the presence of non-voting staff may cause the boardroom to capsize.

BOARDROOM LESSON

The board chair and the CEO should focus on inviting the *right* non-voting staff members into the boardroom at the *right* time and for the *right* length of time.

Board Action Steps:

○ **1. Review:** If non-voting staff members are routinely in the boardroom, is this practice helpful to the board processes? The board may not have considered this question.

○ **2. Evaluate:** The board chair can evaluate the inclusion or exclusion of non-voting board members in the boardroom and discuss the issue during executive session.

○ **3. Communicate:** If the board makes a decision to modify existing practice, clearly communicate the reasons for inclusion and exclusion to the staff. If the board permits staff members in the boardroom, communicate expected behavior.

Prayer
Lord, give us wisdom in determining how and when to utilize the input of staff to the board.
Amen.

PART 4:

EPIPHANIES
IN THE BOARDROOM

People lose their way when they lose their why.[1]

Michael Hyatt

13 | CAUTION! UNDERSTAND THE GOVERNANCE PENDULUM PRINCIPLE

You have limited time to act when the pendulum oscillates in a positive direction.

New [board] members haven't been around long enough to have been affected (or infected) by the board's paradigms. New [members] in their first two years can ask penetrating questions from perspectives that might be quite different from everyone else's.[1]

John Pellowe

Cindi was elected as the second CEO of a ministry, replacing the retiring founder. A few months into her new position, she had made an assessment: several key governance changes were needed.

The board did not have term limits, and many of the board members had served from the beginning of the founder's tenure. There was no Board Policies Manual. Standing committees abounded. The bylaws sorely needed revision.

So Cindi met with the board chair to discuss her observations and quickly learned there was no openness to contemplate her recommendations. Stunned, she couldn't grasp why her governance ideas were not worthy of consideration.

Here's what Cindi failed to understand: governance changes are often inextricably linked to the Governance Pendulum Principle: Opportunities for substantial governance improvement only occur when the governance pendulum oscillates in a positive direction.

In contrast, Ray became the CEO of a ministry that was open to governance changes. The board knew governance improvements were needed. They just lacked the appropriate board leadership and experience to see the changes become reality.

> *Opportunities for substantial governance improvement only occur when the governance pendulum oscillates in a positive direction.*

So in the first two years of Ray's tenure, the board, working closely with the board chair, reviewed and updated the bylaws, revised the board committee structure, and developed their first Board Policies Manual. That resulted in a new and fresh spirit in their board meetings.

The Governance Pendulum Principle is one of the least understood governance concepts. To the novice observer, every board has the potential to experience the swing of the governance pendulum at any time. However, solid progress is rarely possible when the pendulum is in a negative or resting position.

Boards must be alert to three pendulum positions—resting, negative, and positive:

1. **The resting position.** For many boards, the pendulum is in a resting, equilibrium position. The pendulum has not moved in a long time. And without God's help, there is no prospect for it to move. When the pendulum is in the

resting position, some changes are possible, but the changes are probably minor ones.

2. **The negative position.** While positive change rarely occurs during a negative pendulum swing, a negative swing is almost always a precursor to the possibility of positive change. To reverse a negative pendulum swing often requires a new CEO, new board members, and/or a new board chair.

3. **The positive position.** When the pendulum finally oscillates in a positive direction, positive changes are possible. But there is a limited time for the board to act because the board pendulum will eventually return to a resting position. Or worse, the pendulum will swing to a negative position.

> *The status quo is the only condition the [board] cannot veto.*

Here are five significant barriers that prevent a positive swing in the governance pendulum:

1. **Status quo outlook.** Any board can develop a nonprogressive attitude. A board can easily become stuck in the status quo. Though new members on the board may bring fresh ideas, it is often difficult to change the status quo culture of the board. Perhaps your board is like the leader who quipped, "The status quo is the only condition the [board] cannot veto."[2]

2. **Self-appointed progress blockers.** Even if a board is generally inclined to move forward with positive governance changes, just one or two negative board

members can unfortunately, but effectively, block all progress.

3. **No term limits.** A surprising 67 percent of ECFA boards have no term limits, according to ECFA research.[3] Without fresh faces, it is a rare board that is forward-looking in terms of governance. A lack of new members is like being locked in a time warp. Term limits are not a magic potion, but they ensure that board members opposed to progress will eventually exit stage left.

4. **The board is too large.** The larger the board, the more difficult it is to move the pendulum. While there is no magic number, boards greater than 15 are often unwieldy.

5. **Believing the board cannot change.** One of my neighbors recently installed an Invisible Fence. When my wife and I walk by the house, their very large dog barks loudly, runs, and jumps, but he knows where the underground perimeter is and avoids it.

   And so it is with ministry boards. If they *believe* there is a barrier to change, there will typically be no change.

Here are four elements that will have a major impact on effectively moving the governance pendulum to the positive side:

1. **Identifying the governance changes that should be made.** Positive governance changes can occur only in an environment where the potential changes have been identified. A vision for governance improvement is the key to change.

2. **The CEO's openness to change.** It is possible for a board to make substantive governance changes—even if the CEO is not on board with the changes—but it is unlikely to be a congenial process. A CEO who is negative toward the changes will be a drag on positive development.

3. **The board's openness to change.** In our earlier example, Cindi identified needed governance changes. However, the missing element was the board's openness to change. Without the board's concurrence with proposed changes, there can be no forward movement.

4. **Sensing when God is telling the board to change.** Hearing from the Holy Spirit is the most important element in creating positive changes for boards.

It is only with the help of the Lord—and often the Lord uses fresh faces on the board—that a ministry will begin the important process of governance improvement. God can move mountains, so you can also trust Him to move pendulums!

Seeking God's will is necessary to reveal His plan. David sought help from the Lord as he fought the Philistine army. The Lord's response in 2 Samuel 5:24 provided the open door for David: "As soon as you hear the sound of marching in the tops of the poplar trees, move quickly, because that will mean the Lord has gone out in front of you." He will give that same clarity to your board.

William Barclay reminds us: "We are trying not so much to make God listen to us as to make ourselves listen to Him; we are trying not to persuade God to do what we want, but to find out what He wants us to do."[4]

BOARDROOM LESSON

Be encouraged: God moves mountains and pendulums! Opportunities to improve a ministry's governance are limited to certain situations and fleeting time periods. Seize the opportunity for change!

Board Action Steps:

○ **1. Read:** *The Steward Leader: Transforming People, Organizations and Communities,* by R. Scott Rodin, contrasts the stark difference between steward leaders and owner-leaders.[5]

○ **2. Assess:** Conduct an assessment of your board's governance pendulum. Can you point to changes—positive or negative—that the board has made in recent years?

○ **3. Act:** If you sense positive movement in the board pendulum, identify the most important changes that can be made during this window of opportunity.

Prayer
Lord, we have faith that you will move the governance pendulum. We need Your help to improve our governance for the sake of Your ministry.
Amen.

14 | PLANT A SEED IN THE BOARDROOM

Watch the Lord reap the harvest.

Help me remember, God, that I can be reassigned, neutralized,
or eliminated for a thousand different reasons at any moment.
My leadership is precarious, hanging by the silver thread
of people's trust in me. Countless things over which I have
no control can break that thread, including your call elsewhere,
and I will be gone.[1]

Richard Kriegbaum

Paul Nelson was the executive vice president and chief operating officer with Focus on the Family in the mid-1990s. While serving with Focus, Paul was also serving on ECFA's board. During that time, ECFA was in a presidential search, and Paul was on the search committee. The last candidate had been interviewed.

Meanwhile, back in Colorado Springs, Paul had a spiritual experience while visiting the construction site for Focus on the Family's new facility. Each weekend, Paul checked on the construction progress.

On that Sunday afternoon, he climbed the ladder to the top floor of the new building. With Pike's Peak in the background, he surveyed the landscape and the entire architectural layout. From that height, he could see the big picture, and all of the pieces of this project were finally coming together.

Then Paul felt the Spirit stirring his heart, and he found himself praying out loud. In that moment, he sensed that his purpose at Focus was to lead them through the construction of the new building—*and perhaps*—not beyond.

On top of that building, Paul felt a lifting of the mantle for the first time in his nine years at Focus. Why hadn't the search committee been able to find the right candidate for ECFA? Paul talked to his wife, Elaine. They prayed about the opportunity. He asked himself, *If this last candidate for the ECFA president's position turns us down, does that mean I'm the one to move ECFA forward?*

When that final candidate did, in fact, say no to ECFA's invitation, Paul called the search committee chair and said, "I think the Lord is speaking to me. I'd like to resign from the search committee and put my name in for consideration."

Shortly thereafter, Paul was elected ECFA's president and served with excellence for 12 years.

That holy moment began with a seed—planted in the ECFA boardroom—that led to his call to the top leadership post of the ministry. You never know how and when God will use a boardroom experience to speak to the heart of a board member about future service in your ministry.

We plant seeds with givers. We plant seeds with collaborators. We plant seeds here and there in our personal and ministry lives. But rarely do we think about planting seeds in the boardroom.

Sadly, our focus is all too often on how much board members may contribute to the ministry. Or we focus on how much money board members can raise for the ministry. Yet when we over-focus on the money side, we can miss the more significant opportunities for the people God has placed right in front of us.

Few of your board members will ever sense the call to be your ministry's CEO. But consider how the Lord might be prompting them:

- **One might say yes to a future $1-a-year position.** Most ministries never have enough volunteers. Some of your board members may be the volunteers you are looking for somewhere down the line.

- **One might hear God's call to a key staff position.** Perhaps one of your board members might be your future chief operating officer, chief financial officer, or chief development officer.

> *You never know how and when God will use a boardroom experience to speak to the heart of a board member about future service in your ministry.*

- **One might share a ministry opportunity with friends.** Your board members may not be prospects for a volunteer or staff position, but they may have a friend who is just the person you need.

Don't miss those holy opportunities to plant seeds in the boardroom. Invest time in one-on-one meals with board members to help them hear from God. You never know how God will use a story or a few words to bless a board member and the ministry.

BOARDROOM LESSON

The boardroom experience is fertile ground
for planting seeds with board members.
Be alert to ways the Holy Spirit may use those holy moments
to reap a great harvest at a later date.

Board Action Steps:

○ **1. Invest:** Get to know your board members—not just superficially. Really get to know them.

○ **2. Inspire:** Share short-term and long-term ministry opportunities that may have a specific interest to certain board members.

○ **3. Intercede:** Pray that the Lord of the harvest will use those seeds to yield an abundant harvest in His time.

Prayer
Lord, help us to be faithful in planting seeds
in the hearts of board members—
seeds that may sprout months or years later.
Amen.

15 | BE INTENTIONAL ABOUT YOUR FIRST 30 MINUTES

Does your board meeting need a refresh—so you experience holy moments more frequently?

> *How do you refresh a meeting that's grown rote?*
> *Break the script.*[1]
>
> Chip Heath and Dan Heath

It's so ironic. The same Christ-centered ministries that leverage God-honoring creativity at their ministry events often torture their long-suffering board members with boring board meetings.

Imagine if you tasked your creative event team to suggest ways to refresh and enrich your board meetings. What would an inspiring and productive board meeting look like? *How many holy moments can you recall from last year's board meetings?*

Picture this boardroom:

> "James, our esteemed board chair, called last night and asked me to share some spiritual insights tonight. So let me read an interesting piece I found on the internet."

Within moments the board members' eyes glaze over, as it seems the piece isn't so interesting after all.

Of course, it really doesn't matter—because a few people are always late, which also doesn't matter, according to Scott Adams, creator of Dilbert:

Too true! If we're not intentional about the first 30 minutes, Christ-centered governance may often look and taste like most secular meeting models—with one exception: you'll drop in a prayer at the beginning and the end of the meeting; and maybe throw in a devotional thought or poem. Then presto! We think we have achieved "God-honoring governance." *Not really.*

While participating in numerous board meetings and board retreats over the years, we have observed and appreciated the power of preparation—and being at least as intentional about the first 30 minutes of a board meeting as we are about meal choices (steak or salmon?).

Rather than coasting into the agenda (housekeeping items, late starts, false starts, come-to-order preliminaries), thoughtful intentionality by board chairs and CEOs will often command immediate attention and eternity-lasting Kingdom results.

Let's confess. Our board meetings have gotten sloppy when:

✓ Preparation is rote

✓ Execution is rote

✓ Celebration is rote

✓ Follow-through is random

Heed the challenge from Chip Heath and Dan Heath in their 2017 book, *The Power of Moments: Why Certain Experiences Have Extraordinary Impact.* With examples from education, business, hospitality, and church sectors, they call leaders and teams to break out of the routine and defy "the forgettable flatness of everyday work and life by creating a few precious moments."[2]

What if you maximized the first 30 minutes of your board meeting or board retreat with a few precious moments? Imagine this result:

> *Break out of the routine and defy "the forgettable flatness of everyday work and life by creating a few precious moments."*

"How was the board meeting tonight, dear?"

"*Oh, my!* I'll never forget it. We had a holy moment! Here's what happened…"

At one retreat, a short inspirational video launched the meeting. The video helped board members transition from the commuting hassles of arriving at the meeting . . . to the holy calling of being board members/stewards of the ministry. The video sharpened each board member's focus and brilliantly set the spiritual tone for the meeting.

At another board meeting, a board member shared an inspirational two-page presentation that was the catalyst for a major fork-in-the-road decision about the future.

In this case, the board member had clearly taken time to hear from God—to discern what God was saying to him and the board. Then he wrote his presentation, rehearsed it, and with a Holy Spirit-empowered conviction and a stunning use of Scripture, inspired the board to think bigger about its Kingdom calling.

At the conclusion of the meeting (equally as intentional as the beginning), each board member shared their "One Big Take-Away." It was powerful! Many board members mentioned the devotional presentation as the highlight of the board meeting.

Think back over your last few board meetings or last year's board retreat. Can you remember what anyone shared or prayed about? Inspire your board to higher levels of governance and creativity. Remember that our Creator (*talk about creativity!*) said, "It is good." He didn't say, "Oh, it'll do."[3]

BOARDROOM LESSON

What happens at the very beginning of your board meeting signals to everyone the tone and the tenor of the entire meeting. So orchestrate your first 30 minutes to create the expectation that this board meeting has eternal consequences. *How you launch will impact how you land.*

Board Action Steps:

○ **1. Refresh:** Ask a creative team member to help you refresh the first 30 minutes of your board meetings. Suggest he or she read *The Power of Moments* from Chip and Dan Heath.[4]

○ **2. Relate:** Be intentional and prayerful as you invite a board member (or staff member) to share a spiritual insight that will be relevant (not random) to the focus of the board meeting.

○ **3. Reflect:** Create unhurried space at the end of your meeting for around-the-room "One Big Take-Away" responses. (How you launch will impact how you land.)

Prayer

Lord, forgive us for our lack of intentionality.
Forgive us for haphazardly dashing through
our opening half hour—and relegating You
to the preliminaries.
Amen.

16 | LOOKING FOR CONSENSUS BUT FINDING DIVISION

Finding consensus on challenging issues requires deft handling and a flexible approach by the board chair.

A guiding principle is that when the board is making a decision, the process should be fair, open, and recorded.[1]

Robert C. Andringa and Ted W. Engstrom

The board meeting started well, but the first issue on the agenda was a doozy. The ministry was about to launch a major building campaign and three fundraising consultants had submitted proposals. The building committee recommended one of the three firms but without much conviction.

After a brief discussion, it was obvious that the board was deeply divided on the issue. Liz and Rick squared off with passionate speeches, debating pros and cons. Alan and Bill took some cheap shots at each other. The situation was to the point where board members were squirming in their seats.

As one board member after another dug in their heels, uncertainty was written across the face of the chair. But with a motion and a second on the table, the board chair decided to proceed to a vote.

A novice could have predicted what would happen next: a split decision. Eight voted yes and seven voted no. While the motion carried and *Robert's Rules of Order* was followed, the matter had clearly not been handled well. The remainder of the meeting was tension-filled. Not only did the board fail to find consensus, they didn't even find common ground.

Conversely, a colleague tells a story with a much happier ending. Their ministry board was considering the acquisition of a major piece of real estate for a new facility. The matter had been on the agenda for more than six months.

> *The board moved to a stunning level of congeniality and even consensus—thanks to the grace-giving way the board deliberated on this significant decision.*

Every angle from zoning to parking to the mortgage had been carefully analyzed. There was a motion and a second to move ahead with the acquisition. The board chair then went around the table and asked each member to share their feelings on the acquisition. Everyone was ready to move forward except Roger who said he was not comfortable about proceeding.

The board chair could have moved to a vote and the issue would have passed. But he discerned it would be wiser to table the motion until the next meeting. Over the next month, the board chair met with Roger several times to discuss Roger's misgivings. By the time the board met again, Roger had reached a comfort level with the property acquisition and the issue passed unanimously. The result: the board moved to a stunning level of congeniality and even consensus—thanks to the grace-giving way the board deliberated on this significant decision.

What do these two stories tell us? Being the board chair is an extremely challenging task. And there is not one right way to handle every item on the agenda.

Your ministry's bylaws may provide guidance on how the board reaches decisions. Or, it may simply say that the board must follow *Robert's Rules of Order*—a process with which few board chairs or boards are fully conversant.

You have heard the terms *consent agenda, unanimity, simple majority*, and *super majority*. Inherent in all of these terms (which are discussed in more detail below) should be a desire to find consensus—a word that is often not well understood. *Merriam-Webster* defines consensus as, "general agreement or unanimity, the judgment arrived at by most of those concerned, or group solidarity in sentiment and belief."[2] Consensus is a spirit or sense of the board. It is not a formal action. It is a process that seeks widespread agreement among group members. Unanimity is one possible result of the consensus process.

Determining if there is consensus on a particular agenda item before a vote is taken is often an excellent approach. After adequate discussion, the chair asks, "Is there consensus that it's time to vote?" This is a signal: If you have more to add, speak up! At times, a red or green straw vote card may be used to indicate consensus.[3] "If you are ready to vote, hold up your green card; if not, hold up your red card."[4]

The bottom line: your board needs to find a way to reach decisions peacefully, thoughtfully, fairly, and openly. To avoid the wounds of division, your board should agree on the best way to reach consensus. Here are three approaches:

- **A consent agenda.** Routine items can be grouped under one agenda item, termed a consent agenda. These items might include approving the minutes of the previous meeting, committee assignments, committee reports, and the like. Using this approach, the board chair entertains a motion to approve all of the items in the consent agenda. Agenda items upon which the board is unlikely to quickly reach consensus should not be included in a consent agenda.

- **Unanimity.** It is rare for boards to require unanimity (100% agreement) on all actions. The danger in requiring unanimity is that one person can block an action and allow a decision to simply be endlessly kicked down the road. "The practice of required unanimity tends to silence those who would otherwise take a different view unless they think it is of critical importance. Others may feel unspoken pressure to go along with the perceived majority at the time of voting only to feel like a hypocrite later."[5]

  While reaching a unanimous decision is a positive accomplishment, most boards realize that it is acceptable for one or more members to dissent from a decision.

- **Simple or super majority.** Most boards make decisions by simple majority. However, the constitution, or bylaws, or your Board Policies Manual may require more than a simple majority for certain actions, such as the purchase or sale of property. A so-called super-majority usually requires a two-thirds or three-fourths affirmative vote of the board.

To reach consensus peacefully, thoughtfully, fairly, and openly, leverage the five keys:

1. **Right purpose.** The board must always start and finish with the Colossians 3:17 test: "And whatever you do, whether in word or deed, do it all in the name of the Lord Jesus giving thanks to God the Father through Him" (NIV).

2. **Right people.** Unless the right people are around the board table, which involves board selection, orientation, and ongoing training, the seeds are sown for division in the boardroom.

3. **Right board chair.** When it comes to finding consensus, the chair is the key person. (In 16 percent of ECFA boards, according our research, the CEO is also the board chair, but we do not recommend this approach.[6]) For more insights, read David McKenna's masterful book, *Call of the Chair: Leading the Board of the Christ-centered Ministry.*[7]

4. **Right agenda.** A well-planned agenda goes a long way for achieving consensus. Putting the right issues on the agenda at the right time requires discernment.

5. **Right approach.** There is no single right approach for every agenda item in every meeting. Sometimes, while the board meeting is in progress, the chair will sense the Holy Spirit's leading—and call a holy time-out. This might require setting aside usual parliamentary procedures and functioning as a committee-of-the-whole (the board operates as a committee under informal rules). *It may also involve prayer!*

BOARDROOM LESSON

Glorify God in your board meetings
by achieving consensus when possible.
God-honoring decisions can be made
peacefully, thoughtfully, fairly, and openly—
when you have the right purpose, the right people,
the right board chair, the right agenda,
and the right approach.

Board Action Steps:

○ 1. **Reflect:** When divisions have occurred in your decision-making, how has your board chair addressed them?

○ 2. **Review:** Discern how the board can improve its decision-making processes and foster greater congeniality towards reaching a consensus.

○ 3. **Re-visit:** Periodically re-visit the consensus-reaching and decision-making processes and make adjustments as necessary.

Prayer
Lord, thank You for giving us the Holy Spirit
who guides us in making our board decisions.
Amen.

PART 5:

BOARDROOM BLOOPERS

Peter [Drucker] helped me to stop doing things.
Or as he succinctly put it, "When the horse is dead,
dismount." If something isn't working—
or not working as robustly as it once did—
I abandon what I'm doing
and redirect the resources to more promising opportunities.[1]

Bob Buford

17 BOTCHED EXECUTIVE SESSIONS ARE NOT PRETTY

Don't assume that your executive sessions will automatically be excellent.

> *The board speaks with one voice or not at all.*[1]
>
> John Carver

You may have attended one of these not-so-pretty executive sessions. Just before the board meeting concludes, ministry staff are asked to leave the boardroom. Then the board chats with the CEO, followed by the CEO leaving the room.

Next, board members discuss executive session-appropriate topics, such as the CEO's performance and compensation. Occasionally—oops—sometimes they weigh in on topics that should have been discussed before the board went into executive session.

Finally, the board adjourns and everyone departs.

Except the CEO. He or she is left wondering, what was discussed in the executive session—and why did it take so long? The minutes are silent and record just one line: "The board met in executive session."

So what could have been an enriching experience for both the board and the CEO becomes a misguided, amateurish spectacle—another botched boardroom debacle. All CEOs know they don't always bring their A game to their work. The best CEOs are always open to coaching and improvement. And the best boards create a boardroom environment that leverages executive sessions for the good of the CEO and the ministry. In addition, they treat executives with thoughtfulness and God-honoring grace.

Too many boards fail to follow a sound protocol when conducting executive sessions. The board is well intentioned, but they are oblivious to the fact that they are harming their relationship with the CEO.

Here are seven principles for conducting executive sessions of the board:

- **PRINCIPLE 1: An executive session without the CEO should never include issues that are of a non-sensitive nature.** For example, a board discusses CEO performance and compensation in executive session and then veers into topics of a non-sensitive nature, such as changing the location of the next board meeting. *The CEO should have been in the boardroom for the non-sensitive topics.*

> *Too many boards fail to follow a sound protocol when conducting executive sessions. The board is well intentioned, but they are oblivious to the fact that they are harming their relationship with the CEO.*

- **PRINCIPLE 2: A board should always meet in executive session in at least two situations: (1) when considering the CEO's periodic review, and (2) when reviewing the**

CEO's compensation. A review of the CEO may be performed by the board as a whole or by a board committee. After the review has been completed, the board chair or a board committee should discuss the results of the review with the CEO. However, if the entire board discusses the review with the CEO, voting and non-voting staff should be recused from the discussion.

The CEO's compensation will always be reviewed in executive session. The CEO and voting and non-voting staff should not be in the boardroom when the CEO's compensation is being discussed and approved.

- **PRINCIPLE 3: Board meetings should rarely be conducted unless the CEO is included in the meeting.** If a CEO is not invited to a board meeting or a significant portion of a meeting, this almost always indicates the CEO's tenure is in jeopardy. However, an executive session without the CEO is appropriate because the board should discern whether to retain the CEO and/or how to structure a transition for the CEO's departure. Another instance when it is appropriate for the board to meet without the CEO is when the board is involved in a CEO succession planning process.

- **PRINCIPLE 4: The CEO should generally be present at the beginning of an executive session.** This enables the CEO to gain a sense of the topics the board has in focus. Additionally, many questions that board members raise during an executive session can be answered only by the CEO.

- **PRINCIPLE 5: Following an executive session, the gist of the discussion should be communicated to the CEO in a constructive manner.** The temptation is to be comprehensive in telling the CEO every point that came up. But boards should be sensitive about what they tell the CEO, particularly regarding executive performance.

The person presiding over the executive session plays an important role in subsequently delivering feedback to the CEO. The accuracy and honesty of this feedback are crucial. These are delicate matters. The wrong choice of words, the wrong tone, or lack of sensitivity can be very detrimental to the CEO's relationship with the board.

Some boards' policies may require two directors to meet with the CEO to share a summary of the executive session discussion. This practice allows the two directors to cross-check with each other regarding what nuances of the dialogue to convey. It also validates the overall feedback for the CEO.

Other boards invite the CEO to re-enter the boardroom while the entire board is still in session, and the board chair summarizes for the CEO the executive session discussion. This is often awkward since all eyes will be on the CEO, watching for even the slightest reaction, verbal or non-verbal.

Of course, numerous executive sessions are very positive in nature and the report will be an encouragement to the CEO.

- **PRINCIPLE 6: During the executive session, not every comment made by every board member will necessarily be appropriate or substantive.** The person presiding at the executive session should ask for full board affirmation to the core value, "The board speaks with one voice, or not at all."[2] If there is not majority agreement on an issue or topic, it should not be communicated to the CEO, and it should not be discussed by anyone outside of the boardroom.

- **PRINCIPLE 7: If feedback to the CEO is not provided right after the session, it should be conveyed within a day or two so that the discussion is fresh in the minds of board members sharing the report.** Under no circumstances should comments or feedback be attributed to individual board members. Anonymity is of utmost importance.

Executive sessions are excellent only when appropriate topics are discussed and only when there is effective communication with the CEO before, during, and after each executive session. As experienced board members know, it's far too easy to botch what should be a helpful lifelong learning experience for their CEO. Choose excellence!

At the heart of excellent executive sessions are fundamental Christ-centered values, the fruit of the Spirit: love, joy, peace, forbearance, kindness, goodness, faithfulness, gentleness, and self-control (Gal. 5:22-23).

BOARDROOM LESSON

Executive sessions can be extremely productive or very devastating. One of the keys to an effective relationship between the CEO and the board is for boards to strive for excellence when meeting in executive session without the CEO. Pray for wisdom!

Board Action Steps:

○ **1. Schedule:** Establish a pattern for executive sessions. If your board meets monthly, perhaps quarterly executive sessions are appropriate. If the board meets quarterly or less often, perhaps an executive session at the close of each meeting is appropriate.

○ **2. Plan:** Just as the board meeting needs an agenda, an executive session also needs an agenda.

○ **3. Debrief:** After an executive session in which the CEO was excluded, the board chair and perhaps another board member should meet with the CEO in a timely manner to provide the CEO with an overview of the executive session.

Prayer
Lord, we especially need Your wisdom when we meet in executive sessions. And we need the fruit of the Spirit to be active in our lives.
Amen.

18 | WARNING! RESUMÉ-BUILDERS MAKE LOUSY BOARD MEMBERS

He envisioned how board service would look on his resumé.

It is important to point out to prospective candidates
what is expected of them, including the role of active advocate.
Misleading expectations result in nothing but grief.
To tell you the truth, good people don't want
to be part of something that requires little of them.[1]

Max De Pree

Sometimes a board prospect is way too eager to join your board.

When you propose marriage on your first date with a board prospect, you'll usually regret it. This board lesson is a good reminder to slow down and take your time.

Al was the CEO of ABC Ministry. He also served on the board of XYZ International. So Al asked his friend Jordan about his interest in serving on the board. One problem: Al failed to mention which board!

Jordan had always been interested in XYZ International. In fact, he envisioned how board service at XYZ would look on his resumé and his LinkedIn profile. (Maybe he even fantasized about chairing the board someday.)

So the entire dating-a-board-prospect process took no longer than a hallway conversation on the way to lunch. Al asked Jordan to serve on the board, and Jordan was pleased to accept.

On the day of his first board meeting (a Saturday), Jordan arrived early at the XYZ International office. He wasn't that early, but the parking lot was empty. He waited. He waited. He waited—but still no board members. Not even Al, who had talked vaguely about a short orientation session for new board members prior to the board meeting.

> *He envisioned how board service at XYZ would look on his resumé and his LinkedIn profile.*

No need to panic, thought Jordan. He called Al, who answered on the first ring.

"Where are you?" Al asked.

"In the parking lot at XYZ," responded Jordan. "Where is everyone?"

"Oh, no," laughed Al. "Sorry to confuse you. We always hold ABC Ministry board meetings here at our ABC offices. You're just 30 minutes away, if you hurry. We'll start without you, but we're looking forward to welcoming you to the board."

Jordan was stunned. Apparently, he had said yes to serving on the ABC Ministry board, not the XYZ International board. *Oh, my.* Wishing to avoid public embarrassment, Jordan took a big gulp and soldiered on. He served a three-year term on a ministry board for which he had zero passion.

BOARDROOM LESSON

When recruiting board prospects, go slowly. Over-communicate. Introduce the prospects to other board members. Protect your ministry by ensuring that only spiritually and emotionally mature people are invited to be stewards of your organization.

Board Action Steps:

○ **1. Read:** Order the 91-page gem, *Called to Serve: Creating and Nurturing the Effective Volunteer Board* by Max De Pree,[2] for your board, and invite a board member to highlight an insight from it at every meeting.

○ **2. View:** Screen the 13-minute video from the *ECFA Governance Toolbox Series No. 1: Recruiting Board Members* and distribute the *Board Member Read-and-Engage Viewing Guide*[3] at your next board meeting or nominating committee meeting.

○ **3. Review.** Does your board policy require that nominees are interviewed by two or more board members?

Prayer

Lord, forgive us for being slot fillers
when You want us to be Kingdom builders.
As we consider board nominees, forgive our lame
excuses for second-rate work: lack of time,
convenience, procrastination, and half-heartedness.
Instead, lead us to Your candidates for the board.
Amen.

19 | BEWARE THE PHONE-BOOK-SIZE REPORT

My 84-page PDF landed with a thud.

*There is one quality needed in the board leader's essential toolkit:
"a capacity for complete candor and a willingness
to ask the same of others."* [1]

Ram Charan, Dennis Carey and Michael Useem

This boardroom blooper cost me an expensive dinner.

Here's some wisdom from a board expert. I knew the wisdom. I preached the wisdom. I just didn't practice the wisdom. In his *Harvard Business Review* article, "What Makes Great Boards Great," Jeffrey A. Sonnenfeld warns against "phone-book-size" board reports.

> "What kind of CEO waits until the night before the board meeting to dump on the directors a phone-book-size report that includes, buried in a thicket of subclauses and footnotes, the news that earnings are off for the second consecutive quarter? Surely not a CEO who trusts his or her board. Yet this destructive, dangerous pattern happens all the time." [2]

Fortunately, my phone-book-size report did not include bad news. But the size—84 pages—was bad news enough.

Worse, the inexcusable tardiness and size of my report, prepared at the request of the ministry's CEO, made him look bad. The committee members received the email with the 84-page PDF just an hour before the scheduled conference call.

I rationalized my tardy behavior:

- Even if I sent it sooner, they wouldn't have opened the email until 30 minutes before the conference call.

"What kind of CEO waits until the night before the board meeting to dump on the directors a phone-book-size report? Surely not a CEO who trusts his or her board."

- My cover note clearly explained: "No need to read this in advance. We will walk you through the highlights. Background info only!"

Well, the 84-page report landed in the email inboxes of each committee member with a thud.

The committee conference call started on time with all members present. But before the CEO could ask the committee chair to begin the meeting with prayer, an irritated but courteous committee member sounded off.

"Can I just say that receiving an 84-page report less than an hour before our conference call was not appreciated? I didn't have time to review it in this last hour. Can we be sure this doesn't happen again?"

The CEO and committee chair immediately agreed and apologized. They were people of high character and graciousness. They didn't blame me, but they could have.

The committee meeting eventually did go well. Some leaders are very gifted at changing the tone of a meeting from negative to positive. This CEO saved my bacon. *Whew.*

After we exited the conference call, I immediately called the CEO and apologized. "I owe you lunch or dinner—on me. I'm so, so sorry. Will you forgive me for not serving you well?"

He did. We invited our spouses to join us and had a memorable dinner together. I picked up the check and charged it to the line item in my budget titled "I Just Learned Another Expensive Lesson."

Today, reflecting back on that stinging but well-deserved rebuke from the committee member, I was reminded of another insight in Sonnenfeld's article: the soft side of board governance that distinguishes high-quality boards from the rest of the governance rat race. He calls it a "virtuous cycle of respect, trust, and candor,"[3] but, he warns, even that can be broken at any point if there is no authentic appetite for candor.

He adds, "Almost no one wants to be a skunk at a lawn party."[4]

Board members "are, almost without exception, intelligent, accomplished and comfortable with power. But if you put them into a group that discourages dissent, they nearly always start to conform. The ones that don't often self-select out."[5]

The committee member on our conference call gave a gift to all of us that day—candor. He took a risk, but he reasoned that a Christ-centered board or committee meeting should be a safe place to take a risk. It was. Praise God!

BOARDROOM LESSON

Delivering voluminous board reports with inadequate time for board members to read and review is not only inappropriate, it's disrespectful to board members. Establish policies that articulate the timing and frequency of board meeting materials and reports.

Board Action Steps:

○ 1. **Avoid:** Never, ever deliver agendas, reports, and recommendations at the last minute!

○ 2. **Schedule:** Agree in writing on the board's preferred timetable for receiving board agendas, recommendations, and reports. Example: "All materials for a board meeting shall be emailed (or mailed) at least X days before the board meeting." This policy, including the frequency of reports, can be stated in the Board Policies Manual.

Prayer
Lord, thank You for board members
who speak with graciousness but also candor.
Amen.

PART 6:

BOARDROOM TIME-WASTERS, TROUBLEMAKERS, AND TRUTH-TELLERS

The pruning moment is that clarity of enlightenment when we become responsible for making the decision to own the vision or not. If we own it, we have to prune. If we don't, we have decided to own the other vision, the one we called average. It is a moment of truth that we encounter almost every day in many, many decisions.[1]

Dr. Henry Cloud

20 | DON'T BE LATE—OR ANNOYING!

What's worse than fingernails on a chalkboard? A boisterous board member at a prayer meeting.

Leave space for anyone who may want to speak a first time before speaking a second time yourself.[1]

Ruth Haley Barton

There was good news and there was bad news. And, of course, it included a troublemaker.

That's how we described an afternoon board meeting we facilitated. Let's start with the bad news.

Prior to a special meeting focused on the strategic plan, the board gathered first for prayer and discernment. In teams of three around the boardroom, each group quietly discussed several core questions, then prayed together.

There was a substantive spirit of unity—almost an aroma of joyous expectation. That is, until the one latecomer interrupted the holy quietness with a slammed door and his equally annoying (and unnecessary) greetings.

"Hey, everyone! Sorry I'm late! What's going on? You all in groups? Where's my group? Whatcha working on?"

Not quite fingernails on the chalkboard, but close. Proverbs 29:11 (MSG) pegs this person: "A fool lets it all hang out; a sage quietly mulls it over."

The "sweet, sweet spirit in this place" had left the room to be replaced by a boisterous, inconsiderate board member. He joined a group of his own choosing but continued to voice his questions and comments at decibel levels more in tune with a Major League Baseball game.

> *The "sweet, sweet spirit in this place" had left the room to be replaced by a boisterous, inconsiderate board member.*

What's the good news? In spite of Mr. Uncouth, progress was made. Using green (yes) and red (no) straw vote cards,[2] the board weighed in on several dozen initiatives, then prioritized the few that were especially aligned with the organization's mission, vision, and core values.

The board chair was able to tone down Mr. Uncouth by intentionally engaging *all* the board members, especially those who tended to remain quiet, but when given the opportunity, had great insights to share. The result was a fully engaged and unified board.

Bad news: Some board members are clueless, late to meetings, unprepared, and hog the conversation.

Good news: Grace abounds. We can discern how to leverage their gifts anyway, and in the future, we can also conduct more due diligence through reference checks during the board recruitment process. ("How is Sam in a group setting? Is he a good listener? On time? Respectful of others?")

Bad news: When board meetings involve only talking heads, endless reports, and no time for deep engagement, you'll create an expectation of low expectations.

Good news: When you intentionally create time and space in board meetings for all board members to engage, you'll often be blessed with extraordinary insights, wisdom, and spiritual discernment.

BOARDROOM LESSON

Create a board culture that gives your board chair permission to affirm and reprimand both ends of the continuum: expressive and sometimes boisterous board members but also way-too-quiet board members who have wisdom to share.
Strike a balance and bless the board so deep engagement becomes the norm.

Board Action Steps:

○ 1. **Affirm:** Try this at your next board meeting (by prior delegation): Before the gavel signals adjournment time, ask your best listener on the board to go around the room with a brief kudo for each board member's input during the meeting.

> ✓ "Jack, wow! Thanks for your suggestion on the ABC Project. That was so innovative."

> ✓ "Jill, when we were fumbling all over our revised amendments and missing the import of that outreach opportunity, you called us to prayer. Those five minutes of spiritual refreshment may have been the most important five minutes of our meeting."

> ✓ "Alberto, I've noticed that you are always early to our meetings and always helping Guy with the materials, coffee, snacks, and good humor. Your hospitality gifts are a blessing to all of us."

○ 2. **Reinforce:** You get the idea. Reinforce the good news and, Lord willing, you'll have less bad news.

Prayer
Lord, if I'm the boisterous (and maybe annoying)
board member at our table, help me to tone it down.
And if I'm too quiet or too timid too often,
help me recognize Your Holy Spirit nudges to speak up.
Amen.

21 | ALERT! THE ER FACTOR CAUSES VALUE EXTRACTION

Beware of the ER Factor in the boardroom—ego and rivalry.

Board members who desire to be strong-ER, loud-ER, who focus on pow-ER, or want to be a winn-ER are the antithesis of collaboration.[1]

Randy Ross and David Salyers

When recruiting board members, one of the biggest mistakes boards make is to assess people only in the context of their employment. However, people can change dramatically when they get the board member brass ring.

When new board members are chosen, we always hope that the new members will create value in their board work. Yet two possibilities are crystal clear: board members will either create value or extract value. Few will function in the middle of that continuum.

Value creators bring a positive attitude to each board meeting. They check any thoughts of personal agendas at the door and interact with collegiality. They focus on the vision of the ministry and contribute to its fulfillment. Value creators make generous personal gifts to the ministry and identify others who give their resources and volunteer their time. They operate in "growth gear."

Then there are those who extract value in the boardroom. When a board member puts *I* over *us*, value is extracted. Unfortunately, it's a common dysfunction. When a board member extracts value, it will prompt a downward spiral in the boardroom.

This spiral is multiplied by the ER Factor: when a board member competes against others and positions himself or herself over others. This is the opposite of humility. ER is shorthand for two components that are always prominent in value extraction: ego and rivalry.[2]

Ego and rivalry often lead a board member to elevate self over others by posturing oneself as smart-ER, strong-ER, and bright-ER (which essentially implies bett-ER) than others. This creates a competitive atmosphere in the boardroom, where there is a clear winn-ER and a clear los-ER.

When all board members are creating value and making deposits into their good governance accounts, your board will lead at a remarkable level.

How does a board discern whether a new member is a value creator or a value extractor? Ask these eight questions:

❑ 1. Does the board member enter the boardroom with a receptivity to hearing from the Holy Spirit?

❑ 2. Does the board member attend all board meetings and arrive on time?

❑ 3. Does the board member read the pre-board meeting materials and is prepared to discuss them?

❑ 4. When the board member enters into discussion around the table, is it obvious that the board member is a good listener and does not dominate board discussions?

❑ 5. Is the board member respectful of other board members, speaking kindly and with grace even when sharing strongly held opinions and convictions?

❑ 6. In sidebar discussions when the board is in recess, does the board member make deposits into relationships?

❑ 7. Does the board member strictly abide by the ministry's confidentiality policy and affirm the cardinal rule "What happens in the boardroom stays in the boardroom"?

❑ 8. Does the board member focus on policy matters and avoid operational issues?

During every board meeting and between board meetings, board members are either making withdrawals from or making deposits to good governance. When value extraction exceeds or nearly exceeds value creation, a board member is at risk of outliving his or her usefulness to a board.

When all board members are creating value and making deposits into their good governance accounts, your board will lead at a remarkable level.

BOARDROOM LESSON

Board members either add value or extract value.
Instead of ego and rivalry, board members must model
humility and live in growth gear—engaging with truth
through honest evaluation and maintaining
a solution-oriented perspective.
Demonstrating a heart for *we* versus *me*
inspires other board members to do the same.

Board Action Steps:

○ 1. **Read:** Challenge a board member to read and report
on the book *Remarkable!: Maximizing Results through
Value Creation* by Randy Ross and David Salyers.[3]

○ 2. **Reflect:** Thoughtfully (and confidentially) assess your
current board composition to determine if any board
members represent significant value extractors.

○ 3. **Re-align:** If you do have value extractors on your
board, spiritually discern if and how you can inspire
them to become value creators.

Prayer
Lord, help us recruit value creators to the boardroom
and Your work.
Amen.

22 | WHOPPER MISTAKES CAN UNRAVEL YOUR MINISTRY

If stupidity got us into this mess, then why can't it get us out?

We cannot solve our problems with the same thinking we used when we created them.

The board was at the precipice—one of those moments that board members pray will not occur during their board terms.

The ministry had experienced four consecutive years of million-dollar-plus excesses of expenses over revenues. The CEO had failed to control expenses. At the same time, revenues had rapidly declined.

The deficits had pushed the unrestricted net assets (other than net property, plant, and equipment) into a deficit position. In desperation, the board authorized the use of $2 million in giver-restricted gifts to meet operating expenses. Two major givers, upon learning that their gifts had been misdirected, sued the ministry.

Three days before the board meeting—in the wake of all of these events—the ministry's CEO submitted his resignation. And did we mention: *the board had not conducted a CEO annual performance review in many years.*

It was a somber board meeting. There was considerable casting of blame. The roof seemed to be caving in with no way out. The board prayed, but their prayers did not seem to rise above the ceiling.

The board was on the verge of becoming unraveled. You know, when we pull on a thread—and pull and pull—it unweaves what came before.

When a board becomes unraveled, it comes unwound, rapidly splitting apart like separating threads. Too often, a ministry slowly and imperceptibly unravels for several years before the board wakes up to the reality. Max De Pree said it best: "The first responsibility of a leader is to define reality."[1]

Board stupidity—it sounds so cruel, yet it is so accurate—had gotten this ministry into their mess. But the same stupidity would not get them out.

The board had made some whopper mistakes:

- **Whopper Mistake #1: Failure to give oversight to the finances in general.** As the deficits began to accumulate, the board did not make the necessary cuts early or deeply enough to offset the financial bleeding. Their actions trailed what was happening instead of getting in front of it.

- **Whopper Mistake #2: Failure to require accountability from the CEO for balancing the budget.** The board did not call the CEO's leadership into question as the deficits began to pile up. Instead of changing CEOs, they tried to cover up the problems and hope that everything would turn around.

- **Whopper Mistake #3: Failure to provide accountability for restricted gifts.** Borrowing $2 million of restricted funds for operations was the crowning blow. That one act reflected the height of board irresponsibility.

Should the board have just elected a new CEO and moved on? Hardly. It was time to discern God's direction while getting to the bottom of everything that went wrong. Sometimes this may require retaining a consultant to bring fresh eyes, expertise, and hope to the ministry.

What should a board in a situation like this address immediately? Start with four commitments that all reflect foundational issues:

> *When a board becomes unraveled, it comes unwound, rapidly splitting apart like separating threads. Too often, a ministry slowly and imperceptibly unravels for several years before the board wakes up to the reality.*

- **Commitment #1: Conduct CEO annual reviews.** The board let its guard down—and let the CEO down—by failing to conduct a CEO annual performance review. It must commit to do this in the future with its new CEO.

- **Commitment #2: Assess revenue projections.** Why were revenues rapidly decreasing? Has the bleeding stopped, or is there more to come? What is a realistic view of anticipated resources for the next year? Is it time for a more conservative approach in projecting revenues? Is the organizational mission still relevant?

- **Commitment #3: Reduce expenses and address sustainability.** How deep must expenses be cut and in what areas? Is the organization sustainable—even with deep cuts? Is it time to consider merging with another ministry?

- **Commitment #4: Restore restricted gift balances.** The board must develop a strategy to replace the restricted resources that were inappropriately expended for operational purposes. This should be accomplished in the shortest reasonable time. The board should also adopt a policy of not using restricted gift funds for purposes other than those that the givers intended.

Once these issues are addressed, then it is time to consider who is qualified to lead a turn-around of this ministry. Not every successful leader is skilled in turnarounds, according to Michael Watkins.[2]

When a ministry becomes unraveled, it is not time for rash action. It is time to step back and review how it happened, determine corrective steps, and move ahead—all with the help of the Almighty.

BOARDROOM LESSON

If your ministry becomes unraveled,
it likely did not happen quickly.
Correcting the problems will take time and God's help.
You must identify the whopper mistakes
and make immediate course correction commitments.

Board Action Steps:

○ 1. **Lament:** On the worst day of your board's life, take time to seek God's help.

○ 2. **Learn:** Determine the lessons to be learned from the ministry's challenging experiences.

○ 3. **Legislate:** Take corrective action, including policy revisions, to ensure that there is no repeat of the past.

Prayer
Lord, help us to look to You for guidance both in the good times and when life unravels.
Amen.

23 | THE BULLY IN THE BOARDROOM

The board chair, the CEO, and other board members must neutralize the board bully.

It was more than a little bit helpful to keep the phrase "created in the image of God" in the back of my mind as I listened to someone criticize me or my policies.[1]

Gov. Bill Haslam

A board bully is one who manipulates, pressures, blames, and coerces people to follow his or her ideas or agenda (for example, see what happened to Peter in Galatians 2:12).

Board bullies wreak havoc and create dissension. They often maneuver into leadership positions, such as the chair of an important board or committee. Amazingly, some bullies can even do damage without holding a leadership role.

Thom Rainer[2] and Joe McKeever[3] both describe board bullies with the following characteristics:

1. **They have strong personalities.** They tend to be boisterous. They speak up frequently in meetings and dominate conversations.

2. **They are highly opinionated.** And if you ever disagree with them, you become their next target.

3. **They are famous for using the phrase, "People are saying . . ."** The full sentence could be, "People are saying that you are too critical of your staff." "People" is never defined. The true complainer is never identified.

4. **They are not good listeners.** They want you to listen to them, but they don't want to listen to you.

5. **They do not recognize themselves as bullies.** Instead, they see themselves as heroes sent to save the ministry.

Here's what your ministry can do to minimize the negative impact of board bullies:

1. **Treat the board bully as a person for whom Christ died.** How we treat the board bully "in conversation or [how we] behave toward them in public is a testimony of how Christ would deal with them. We must model respect, love, and compassion in all our words and deeds—as He did."[4]

How we treat the board bully "in conversation or [how we] behave toward them in public is a testimony of how Christ would deal with them. We must model respect, love, and compassion in all our words and deeds—as He did."

2. **Appoint or elect individuals to key positions with care.** Since a board bully generally needs an official pulpit (perhaps that would make it a "bully pulpit"), be careful not to appoint or elect bullies to positions of power.[5] Use a spiritually and strategically designed process to choose and recruit people for key leadership positions.

3. **Pray the bully out of power.** Pray. Ask the Lord for insights. Listen to Him. Wait on Him. Ask prayer warriors

to daily pray a hedge of protection around you and, yes, even ask for prayer that the issues with the bully will be resolved.

4. **Use spiritual discernment in conflict resolution.** Applying spiritual discernment will generally mean holding the bully accountable for what he or she is doing. In extreme cases, bring in help from outside the board to form an intervention team.[6]

5. **Empower your board chair to take appropriate steps in dealing with a board bully.** If the board bully is the board chair—well, that is a big challenge! Otherwise, the board chair should exercise authority in board meetings to assure that the board bully is kept in check.

6. **Be a high-expectation ministry.** "Higher-expectation ministries tend to be more unified, more Great Commission focused, more biblically defined, and more servant oriented."[7] High expectations provide an environment where bullying is ineffective.

7. **Be willing to let the bully leave the board.** Board bullies will often threaten to leave if they don't get their way. In considerate ways, open the door for them. When they threaten to resign, graciously respond, "I accept your resignation."

Not all boards have bullies. Thank the Lord! Once in a while, there are multiple board bullies. When a bully is encountered, the CEO and the board must be on alert and take action to minimize the bully's impact. And, if the CEO is the bully, may heaven help you!

BOARDROOM LESSON

Fundamentally, bullying is a spiritual issue:
you must address the bully in your boardroom—
or the work of God's Kingdom will be hindered.
Board bullies wreak havoc and they create dissension,
yet remember that they are created in the image of God.
Empower your board chair to courageously and graciously
help the bully to exit with grace
or to change his or her sinful pattern.

Board Action Steps:

○ 1. **Commit:** Before your relationships are damaged by a bully in your boardroom, agree—in advance—that the board chair will address the issue.

○ 2. **Care:** As your board chair, accompanied perhaps by another board member, prepares for the "crucial conversation"[8] with the board bully, apply equal doses of spiritual care and biblical discipline, according to Matthew 18.

○ 3. **Complete:** Don't let the problem fester. Find a God-honoring solution. This may be asking the bully to exit.

Prayer
Lord, give us the courage and grace
to address the bully in our boardroom.
Amen.

PART 7:

BOARDROOM
BEST PRACTICES

Whatever the spiritual benefits of our retreat time,
we must always remember that these blessings are not only
for ourselves but for the sake of the communities we belong to—
our families, circles of friendship, our churches, society at large.
The experience of God pours loving energy into us,
qualifies us to serve others with charm and delight.[1]

Emilie Griffin

24 | SHOULD MOST STANDING COMMITTEES STAND DOWN?

How many standing committees are needed for effective governance?

Our board used the same committee structure from year to year with little thought given as to what the committees do or whether they were still relevant to the ministry. We had gotten into a deep rut.

One ministry board fell in love with standing committees. Their CEO loved them too. To make matters worse, the board embedded a generous number of standing committees in the bylaws. Every time a significant issue arose, they added another standing committee.

Some of the standing committee members were current board members, past board members, or individuals who had never served on the board. The CEO was an ex officio member of each standing committee. One or two staff members also served on many standing committees on an ex officio basis.

Because of the complex network of committees, the board spent an inordinate amount of time scheduling committee meetings, attending committee meetings, appointing board members to the various committees, obtaining reasonable attendance at the committee meetings, and more.

The committees were fond of assigning research projects to staff. As a result, staff spent hundreds of hours each year studying issues that rarely ever resulted in committee action, let alone board action.

This all falls under the heading of a standing committee nightmare.

Here are a few key questions and answers:

- **How many standing committees should a board have?** Standing committees are those committees that a ministry uses on a continual basis. They can be established in the ministry's bylaws, in its Board Policies Manual, or in certain other ways.

A good rule of thumb is the fewer standing committees, the better. Only use a committee if it adds value. That tends to push work upward to the full board, which addresses two of the oldest complaints about boards: no substantive agenda items and boring meetings.[1]

The number of board-level committees a ministry should have depends upon many variables, including the age, type, and size of your ministry. Larger ministries tend to need and have more standing committees than smaller ministries.

A start-up or very small ministry may not need any standing committees. If an audit has not yet been performed for the ministry, no audit committee is needed. If the board is small—for example, five or six members— the board itself may care for the work of what a governance committee would do.

- **Which standing committees are most often used by boards?** An executive committee is the most common. However, if the board meets monthly, there is rarely a need for an executive committee to serve between board meetings. Other popular committees are a finance/audit committee for reviewing finances and the audit, and a governance committee, with the responsibility to recommend new board members and to recommend revisions or additions to the Board Policies Manual.

- **When should ad hoc committees and task forces be used?** Ad hoc committees and task forces are the most under-used board tools. They are formed for a limited period of time to address a specific need. Ad hoc committees or task forces are often formed to amend the bylaws, recruit a new CEO, develop a strategic plan, relocate the ministry, or form a new subsidiary.

  > *Ad hoc committees and task forces are the most under-used board tools.*

  Do not form a task force until and unless the board can clearly define a charter for its assignment. Without specificity, a task force may waste the precious time of board members with no measurable achievement.

  When the work of the ad hoc committee or task force is completed, the committee or task force is dissolved. An ad hoc committee or task force may exist for less than a year or for a year or more depending on the extent of the work assigned to it.

- **What can a board do when excessive standing committees are required by the ministry bylaws?** Bylaws can be amended. A board should not feel locked into bylaws that require too many committees. However, it is better to outline standing committees in the Board Policies Manual because the manual can be changed much more easily than the bylaws.

- **How often should a board review its committee structure?** At least every few years, the board should look at the current committee structure and what the committees actually do. If there are overlapping responsibilities or limited work is being done, then it is time to realign the committee structure. Committees with no work should be abolished, and committees with overlapping work should be merged. Committees should not take on a life of their own, nor should they overshadow the board itself.

> *If there are overlapping responsibilities or limited work is being done, then it is time to realign the committee structure.*

Each board must determine the committee structure that works best for the organization. The committee structure should be flexible and meet the changing needs of the ministry. There are a variety of options to choose from, and boards should be willing to experiment. Keep in mind that committees are meant to be tools boards use to get their work done. The right tool for today may not be the right tool for tomorrow. The challenge is in knowing which tool is best for the task at hand.

BOARDROOM LESSON

Boards should use task forces and committees appropriately
as tools to get jobs done while remaining flexible
and diligent about the longevity and function of each group.

Board Action Steps:

○ 1. **Ensure:** Review your board committee structure to ensure that each committee is functioning effectively.

○ 2. **Maximize:** Modify the committee structure as needed in order to maximize the efficiency of the board.

○ 3. **Use:** Consider the use of a task force or ad hoc committee for assignments of a short-term nature.

Prayer
Lord, thank You for our board members
who faithfully serve as committee members,
and help us to maximize the effectiveness
of the committee and task force structure.
Amen.

25 | COMPENSATING THE CEO—IT'S ABOUT MORE THAN MONEY

Getting the compensation-setting process right must be a priority.

When CEO compensation-setting is given an appropriate priority, a ministry board has demonstrated leadership in a significant element of governance.

Anthony has been the ministry's CEO for 15 years. Finances have been tight over this time period. The board has reviewed and adjusted his compensation package about every three years. Even then, the adjustments only amounted to cost-of-living increases.

While there is some unrest on the board about Anthony's performance, it has been five or six years since his last performance review by the board. Since performance reviews and compensation reviews go hand in hand, it is past time for the board to step up to its responsibilities.

Reviewing and setting the CEO's compensation may be one of the board's least favorite things to do. It requires communication with the CEO on a very sensitive topic. It requires obtaining appropriate comparative data. It may require an "out-of-body" experience for most boards—especially if finances are tight.

Boards would rather approve new programs, review the annual audit, adopt new policies—anything but set the CEO's compensation.

Board members from the business world understand the compensation-setting process in that sphere. Leaders of other ministries know how compensation is set in their world. But the compensation-setting responsibilities for your board are often different from other experiences.

> *Boards would rather approve new programs, review the annual audit, adopt new policies—anything but set the CEO's compensation.*

There are so many questions for which there are often unclear answers. Here are ten questions many boards ask:

1. How often should the board obtain compensation comparability data?

2. What is the best source of comparability data?

3. How often should a compensation consultant be used?

4. What types of fringe benefits are appropriate?

5. How much should be allocated to each of the fringe benefit categories?

6. Should there be a compensation framework that considers the relationship between the CEO's pay and the lowest paid position in the ministry?

7. How does founder status or a long versus short tenure figure into compensation planning?

8. What if this is a startup ministry with very limited resources?

9. Should the CEO play any part in the compensation-setting process?

10. Should the compensation increase for the CEO relate to how the ministry is doing financially?

While all of these questions cannot be answered here, there are six principles that boards should consider:

1. **Ensure that the CEO's compensation is reasonable.** The definition of unreasonable compensation is quite illusory. Since compensation is rarely excessive, ministries should more keenly focus on the compensation approval process more than on unreasonable compensation.

2. **Annually review all elements of the CEO's compensation.** Too often, the board focuses on base salary to the exclusion of fringe benefits. All elements of compensation should be considered, including fringe benefits— (taxable, non-taxable, or tax-deferred) such as health insurance and retirement.

3. **Limit the CEO's role in the process.** It is a good plan for the board to discuss the adequacy of compensation with the CEO. Beyond that, the CEO should not participate in the compensation-setting process.

4. **Be informed about the compensation of family members.** While the board would rarely approve the compensation of ministry-paid members of the CEO's

family, the board should be aware of those compensation packages.

5. **Use comparability data.** In some instances, compensation data is not readily available. However, with research, some comparability data can be determined.

6. **Approve the compensation.** Various processes are used to arrive at the compensation level. Here are the key options:

   ☐ **Board as a whole.** For a small ministry with only a few board members, it may make sense for the entire board to handle the compensation-setting process.

   ☐ **Board committee.** A committee of the board may do the initial work on the compensation-setting process with final approval by the full board. This may be the executive committee or another committee.

   The compensation package may be recommended by a board committee, but the ultimate decision on the package should generally be made by the full governing board.

CEOs, and the constituents of ministries, will deeply appreciate boards that address compensation-setting with integrity and thoroughness. Ministries that do not compensate their CEO adequately will be guilty of underpaying their current CEO and will have to play catch-up when setting the compensation of their next CEO.

As your board engages in the compensation-setting process, other resources you may find helpful include:

- ECFA Knowledge Center at *ECFA.org*

- Tax and Financial Guides from ECFA
- Essentials eBook series on *ECFA.org*
- ECFA Standard 6: *www.ECFA.org/Content/Comment6a*

BOARDROOM LESSON

When a board focuses primarily on the cash compensation paid to the CEO, it can easily overlook an equally important element— the process by which compensation is set.

Board Action Steps:

○ 1. **Review:** Annually review the CEO's compensation and fringe benefits package.

○ 2. **Compare:** Obtain periodic comparability data to ensure that compensation is reasonable.

○ 3. **Document:** Approve all elements of the compensation package with the CEO recused and contemporaneously document the board's decision.

Prayer
Lord, we pray for the wisdom to give
adequate attention to the CEO
compensation-setting process.
Amen.

26 | BIG ROCKS, PEBBLES, AND SAND

Ministry boards have a natural gravitational pull toward issues that should be reserved for the staff.

The board is to hold the [ministry] to its biblical ministry direction . . .
The problem for [ministries] is that they tend to get lost
in the minutiae and thus are sidetracked from their mission.[1]

Aubrey Malphurs

Stephen Covey, in *First Things First*,[2] tells the story about a seminar instructor, a gallon jar, fist-sized rocks, small pebbles, sand, and water. The seminar instructor placed the fist-sized rocks in the jar until seemingly full, and then asked the obvious question, "Is that jar full?" The quick answer was yes, but then the instructor proceeded, in turn, to add in smaller pebbles, which easily fit around the rocks, and then sand, which fell through the cracks. Eventually, water was added, and there was room for all of the elements, large and small.

The instructor asked, "What's the point of the illustration?" Someone said, "Well, there are gaps, and if you really work at it, you can always fit more into your life." The instructor quickly responded, "No, that's not the point. The point is this: if you hadn't put these big rocks in first, would you have gotten any of them in?"[3] Applying this illustration to ministry boards, if you haven't identified the big rocks, and instead allow the jar (the agenda) to be filled first with pebbles, sand, and water, the board will miss the opportunity to focus on the major issues.

Think back over the last several board meetings you attended. Count the number of "big rocks" that the board considered in those meetings. If you can't think of many "big rock" issues that were discussed, this suggests that the board probably dealt mostly with minutiae that would have been better left off of the agenda.

Big rocks for your ministry board to address could include: mission, vision, values, the spiritual health of your ministry, major program evaluation (drop, keep, add), facility enhancement or replacement for more than "X" dollars, and how you measure Kingdom results and outcomes. Big rocks might also include planning assumptions about the budget— and how budget performance is monitored, and much more.

Pebbles and sand are the ministry's operational issues, staff supervision, specific ministry plans or strategies, and details that other people should handle. Follow the basic rule of delegating everything possible to the ministry staff.[4]

Ministry boards do not have to handle every rock—only the big rocks! When you see a rockpile, you can be assured that you are seeing the largest rocks in the pile. This is because the smaller rocks, pebbles, and sand have sifted toward the bottom of the pile. If rocks, pebbles, and sand are analogous to the various issues that ministries must address, they are all important at some level, but it's just the big rocks that should be on the agenda of the board.

Know that your board, in all likelihood, would welcome "big rock" agendas. According to ECFA research, 91 percent of board members "understand their role and God's role in goal setting and kingdom outcomes." Further 96 percent of board members agree that "our board understands the core programs, products and services of the organization." Are they ready for you to unleash them on some big rocks?[5]

So, how does a ministry board target the big rocks and allow the staff and volunteers to handle the smaller rocks, pebbles, and sand? Here are five essential governance concepts:

1. **Start with a sound governance philosophy.** It starts with a governance philosophy at the CEO and board chair level (of course, if the CEO is the board chair, we have narrowed the responsibility to one person). The board chair, vice chair, and CEO must build into the board's DNA a stewardship conviction that big rocks are their focus. If not done with intentionality, minor issues will inevitably tempt board members to build sand castles—not Kingdom structures.

   Is there a "glass ceiling" that impedes God's work in your organization? Many smaller ministries fail to grow because their boards are populated with pebble-pickers! *We know. We know.* It is very challenging to move a board from a sand and pebbles mindset to a robust big rocks mentality. But you must do it, with God's grace.

2. **Enforce the big rocks philosophy.** During the meeting, the board chair must be alert for small rocks, pebbles, and sand finding their way onto the table.

Beware the board member who sidetracks a big rocks discussion by dragging you into the sand! Or, someone may introduce a motion that deals purely with operational matters. Either way, the board chair must have the courage to gracefully move the meeting back to focusing on the big rocks. A big rocks philosophy will be nullified without continual enforcement and reinforcement.

3. **Develop a big rocks agenda.** The big rocks philosophy must be evident in the board agenda. If the board agenda includes smaller rocks, pebbles, and sand, there is no hope (or time!) for the board to focus on big rocks. The agenda will drive the focus of the meeting. And the use of a so-called "open agenda," where board members can suggest agenda items "on the fly," will inevitably take the board onto the sand dunes or into sand traps!

   If you decide there are no big rocks to address at the next board meeting, perhaps it is time to consider moving to a less frequent meeting schedule.

   This is where collaboration on the agenda is so important. This is a wonderful opportunity for the CEO and the board chair to meet and identify the big rocks to be considered at the next board meeting. If the CEO is the board chair, the CEO can meet with the vice chair to map out the agenda. If the two leaders decide there are no big rocks to address at the next board meeting, perhaps it is time to consider moving to a less frequent meeting schedule.

4. **Encourage all board members to "sound the alarm" when the discussion goes too far off topic.** Protecting the board ship from running aground on a sandbar should not always be left to the board chair. Any board member should have the courage to adjust the sails when another board member is taking the meeting into minutiae.

When individual board members develop the practice of recognizing and tactfully "calling out" the pebbles and sand problem, it will encourage the board chair to be mindful of these issues.

5. **Refine—don't design.** The boardroom is not an appropriate or effective venue to design programs or address complex issues from scratch. Boards are much better at responding to recommendations from staff or a task force than crafting a plan from zero. Let the staff design and the board refine.

Ministry growth alert! It is very difficult for a ministry to grow beyond the small nonprofit "glass ceiling" unless it gives up a pebbles and sand approach in the boardroom. *Reason:* Focusing on minutiae destroys a board's focus on the most significant Kingdom issues.

BOARDROOM LESSON

Ministries of all sizes must inspire their boards
to address big rocks—substantive Kingdom agenda items—
and create "minutiae-free zones"
where "pebbles and sand" topics are eliminated.
Alert! As ministries grow, the need for boards
to focus on big rocks multiplies exponentially!

Board Action Steps:

○ 1. **Review:** Review your board minutes for the last 12 months. What percentage of the items covered in these meetings represent "big rocks" compared to smaller rocks?

○ 2. **Plan and commit:** If smaller rocks, pebbles, and sand frequently appear on the agenda of past board meetings, decide what it will take to move board deliberations to a higher level. Commit to make the changes necessary to keep the focus on the big rocks.

○ 3. **Re-evaluate:** At least once every six months, evaluate whether the commitment to focusing on major issues is occurring. If not, return to action step #2.

Prayer

Lord, thank You for the wisdom that you give us
to keep our attention on issues that truly matter in the
life of the ministry. Give us courage—and grace—
to avoid living in the land of board minutiae.
Amen.

27 | ADDRESS ABSENTEE BOARD MEMBER SYNDROME

There are three unhealthy ways that many ministry boards respond to empty chairs at board meetings.

I want to manage the [ministry] to God's glory.
Anything less contradicts the Creator, who after creation
surveyed his work and said, "It is good." He didn't say, "Oh, it'll do." [1]

Don Cousins

Which statement below best characterizes your board's response to absentee board members?

- **HO HUM.** Certain board members frequently miss board meetings, but there is no board policy addressing absenteeism, so nothing is said.

- **HINT.** When board members miss a meeting, the board chair (or CEO) gently "hints" that their participation was missed, but nothing further is said. Expectations on board meeting attendance are not clear and are not in writing.

- **HARASS.** If there is a written policy, one willing soul on the board agrees to remind the absentee board member of the policy (usually with a strongly-worded email), but there is no follow-through or personal meeting with the person.

Maybe your board responds more appropriately. We hope so. But if not, here's our list of seven insights for addressing Absentee Board Member Syndrome:

- **Insight No. 1: Recruit committed and faithful people.** It goes without saying (but we're saying it anyway) that you can address 99 percent of future absenteeism problems by focusing on the front end of the board member recruitment process. *Simply recruit people who have already demonstrated high commitment and faithfulness in their previous volunteer and board responsibilities.* Invite people to serve who already have a track record of excellent board meeting attendance in other organizations and settings. And only consider individuals who limit their service to one or two boards at a time (see Lesson 10). Just as you expect your CEO to check references when hiring staff, so the board must carefully check references of board nominees.

- **Insight No. 2: Inspire board members with an annual affirmation commitment.** Leverage a recommitment time each year (a holy moment) with an annual affirmation statement. (Download a template from the *ECFA Governance Toolbox Series No. 1: Recruiting Board Members,*[2] *ECFA Tools and Templates for Effective Board Governance,*[3] or ECFA's Knowledge Center.) That form should list board meeting dates (and key agenda items) for the next 12 to 18 months. It also reminds board members, annually, that if their schedules don't align with the board's schedule—perhaps due to new responsibilities at work or home—they have the option of exiting off the board before their terms are completed. (Or, that discussion might prompt the board to change the meeting dates to accommodate all board members.)

- **Insight No. 3: Engage the board with an engaging agenda.** Sometimes board members skip meetings because they are not needed. The CEO and the staff do all the talking. Next steps are all buttoned down. There's no room for generative thinking by the board. No heavy lifting. No big rocks. What's the point of participating? This is easy to fix by engaging the board in creative ways. (See Lesson 26.)

- **Insight No. 4: Establish a written policy on board meeting attendance requirements.** If you have a Board Policies Manual (see Lesson 4 in *Lessons From the Nonprofit Boardroom*[4]), include board member attendance policies—and review them at least annually. Some boards have an automatic exit plan for board members who miss X meetings in any rolling 12-month period.

> *Sometimes board members skip meetings because they are not needed. The CEO and the staff do all the talking.*

- **Insight No. 5: Emphasize calling over rule-keeping.** Al Newell, founder of High Impact Volunteer Ministry Development, writes: "Sustaining motivation is better understood as a by-product as opposed to a goal of itself. It is my experience that if you pursue discipleship with volunteers [and board members], motivation will follow. If volunteers see the fulfillment of their role as 'obeying and serving God' rather than serving you or your [ministry], it will cause motivation to swell."[5]

- **Insight No. 6: Affirm. Affirm. Affirm.** Take time to creatively affirm board members for their participation and their contribution as stewards of your ministry. Board discipline (news flash!) is the board's responsibility—not the CEO's responsibility. Ditto affirmation. When board colleagues affirm each other, then engagement will heighten and board service satisfaction will soar.

- **Insight No. 7: Address issues early.** Don't wait for the fifth missed meeting. Establish the expectation that your board chair (and perhaps one other board member) will meet personally with policy offenders. No one should be surprised that absenteeism will be addressed when necessary and in a God-honoring way. Pray for a discerning spirit to know when you must show grace— and when you must show someone the door.

BOARDROOM LESSON

Engage the board with an engaging agenda.
When unhealthy attendance patterns arise,
don't respond with unhealthy actions
(Ho Hum, Hint, or Harass).
Instead, address Absentee Board Member Syndrome
early and often.

Board Action Steps:

○ 1. **Engage:** Distribute an engaging agenda prior to the meeting that communicates "Your wisdom and insights are needed."[6]

○ 2. **Ensure:** Verify that you have written policies on board member attendance—and make those clear in the recruitment and onboarding process.

○ 3. **Expect:** Create a boardroom culture and expectation that empowers the board chair to quickly address unexcused absences.

Prayer
Lord, thank You for every board member
and the time each person invests in this holy calling.
Give us courage—and grace—to address
unhealthy board meeting attendance issues.
Amen.

PART 8:

BOARDROOM
WORST PRACTICES

To avoid the potential conflicts of the Successor chair
or the Exemplar chair, many organizations opt for the
Rotator chair. As in the game of musical chairs, members of
the board scurry for the open seat when their turn comes.
The term of the Rotator chair is usually as short as a year or two.
The idea is that the ministry can survive incompetence
for a short period of time.[1]

David L. McKenna

28 | DEFENDING RISKS EVERYWHERE IS NOT A STRATEGIC PLAN

You must discuss the risk elephant in the boardroom.

> *He who defends everywhere, defends nowhere.*[1]
>
> Sun Tzu

Every organization has and takes risks—and ministries are no exception. Neil Simon once said, "If no one ever took risks, Michelangelo would have painted the Sistine floor."[2]

But ask ministry board members to name the top three risks facing the ministry they serve, and their responses will be varied. While many risks will be projected, few board members are prepared to crisply identify the highest risks.

Interestingly, when an ECFA research project compared boards that described themselves as effective to those that are ineffective, 84 percent of effective boards agreed that "Our board devotes creative energy and board meeting time to assess risks and opportunities—and thus is well-informed about the outside forces impacting the organization." Sadly, only 39 percent of ineffective boards agreed.[3]

We know a ministry board that doesn't have term limits for board members. If you were once elected to the board, you are a lifer. So after several years of committee meetings discussing the adoption of term limits, the topic finally makes it to the board agenda. It is a contentious issue because several individuals have been board members for decades and they do not want to give up their positions.

The debate ebbs aimlessly. Then, at a tension-filled moment in the discussion, Ray says he believes the discussion on term limits should be tabled. He contends the ministry has a significant risk because the ministry's physical security policies are out-of-date and the board should focus on security risks.

Most boards do not regularly focus on risks because the topic is generally not on the board's agenda.

Jordan is the board chair, and this isn't his first rodeo. He graciously thanks Ray for his comment on security but suggests that the comment does not really relate to the topic of the hour. The board continues to discuss term limits.

The board adopts the term limit proposal after 90 minutes of discussion, and miraculously the vote is unanimous. Jordan pauses to offer a prayer of thanksgiving for the board's unity.

After he says "Amen," Ray again brings up his concerns about the risk of inadequate security procedures. He is upset that security policies never make it to the board agenda. And, if the policies are a board-level and not a staff-level issue, Ray has a good point.

Why is it so difficult for boards to discuss and identify significant risks? There are several reasons:

- **Failure to put risks on the agenda.** Most boards do not regularly focus on risks because the topic is generally not on the board's agenda. This leaves the door open to the ad hoc management of risks. The risk management topic should be on the board's agenda at least annually.

- **Assuming we have no major risks.** Some boards falsely assume that the ministry does not have any major risks. There are almost always major risks. Boards often identify some routine problems and totally miss the risk elephant in the room.

  Peter Drucker said, "Fortunately or unfortunately, the one predictable thing in any organization is the crisis. That always comes."[4]

- **Treating all risks equally.** Heed the Russian proverb: "If you chase two rabbits, you will not catch either one."[5] If all risks are considered to be equal, then all risks will get the same attention—the major risks and the minor risks. The major risks receive too little attention and the minor risks get too much attention. Few ministries have the resources to fully address every risk.

- **Not adequately considering input from staff.** Boards tend to focus on their own assessment of risks and input from consultants, forgetting that the staff may have keen insights on potential risks. Staff work with organizational systems and volunteers every day. And staff are probably in the best position to assess risks and recommend solutions.

Boards that do not take a proactive approach to risk management are destined to pay a high price when risks make a surprise visit. It is not a matter of whether a ministry has risks; rather, it is a matter of how many risks exist and which ones are significant.

Categories of Risk

Consider these areas when prioritizing possible risks in your ministry. *Note: This list is not exhaustive, but can be a springboard for your discussions. Be sure to get feedback from staff and volunteers on possible risks that the board may not be aware of and prioritize accordingly.*

Category of Risk	Examples
Cybersecurity	Data breaches Malware, spyware
Property	Trip and fall Loss through fire, theft, or natural disaster Vehicles
Human Resources	Regulatory noncompliance Hiring competencies Succession planning
Legal	Lawsuits Contracts
Financial	Fraud Economy/Lack of reserves Budget deficit/borrowing from restricted funds
Givers	Changing giver base Changing giving methods Dependence on limited number of givers
Children	Safety and security Youth safety (travel, activities)
Reputational	Sexual misconduct Appearance of impropriety
Emergency	Active shooter Medical emergencies

BOARDROOM LESSON

Boards are well served to take a holistic approach to risk management, moving from a fragmented view of risks to an integrated and broadly focused view. This approach includes not only risks associated with unintended losses but also financial, strategic, operational, and other risks.

Board Action Steps:

○ 1. **Review:** Regularly include risk assessment on the board's agenda.

○ 2. **Prioritize:** Identify the most important risks and subsequently review the risks to be sure they remain the top risks.

○ 3. **Budget:** Allocate appropriate budgetary funds to address the largest risks.

Prayer
Lord, give our board the discernment
to identify our most significant risks,
and then help us to address them.
Amen.

29 | THE TWO ENEMIES OF SOUND BOARD DECISIONS

Avoid being pressed for time and making major decisions remotely.

Many board meetings would be more productive
if more attention were given to the setting of the meeting
and the time allocated for the meeting.

Two national Christ-centered ministries of significant size began to consider an organic merger. After getting serious about the details, a merger plan was determined and approved by the respective organizations. (It is a truly rare time when an organic merger happens.) It was my privilege to serve on the first board of the newly minted entity.

Each of the organizations coming into the merger owned extensive facilities in different cities. It was inevitable that an early post-merger decision was whether to make one of the existing facilities or a different facility in a third city the eventual home of the new entity.

Board members were notified that the decision on the location of the new entity would be made at an upcoming meeting—a meeting to be conducted by conference call. My immediate reaction to the mode chosen for the important meeting was un-B-E-lievable!

The time allotted for the meeting just added insult to injury. The meeting was limited to one hour. To say I was dubious about how the meeting would be conducted was a gross understatement.

The day and hour for the meeting arrived and I was dutifully on the telephone. The topic was introduced, and speeches were made pro and con, with several board members trying to get the attention of the board chair all at the same time. It was awkward.

The one-hour time quickly passed. Board members were still wanting to be heard. But alas, the 60 minutes were up, and the board chair said there would be no more opportunities for speeches because the board was pressed for time.

> *The discussion was rushed. There was no time to hear from all board members, let alone hear from the Lord.*

The vote was taken. The decision was announced. The meeting was over. There was the "click-click-click-click-click" as members went off the line.

One after another, board members left the call with a knot in their stomachs. Why? It was a huge decision. There was inadequate time for deliberation. The discussion was rushed. There was no time to hear from all board members, let alone hear from the Lord.

How did this happen? How could it have been prevented? What is the impact of a very important decision made in this fashion?

Let's address the first question: how did this happen? The two largest mistakes were:

- **A poor mode was chosen for a very important meeting.** A conference call is rarely a good method for considering a significant decision.

- **An overly restrictive time limit was placed on an important meeting.** The time allocated to a major decision should be consistent with the relative importance of the decision.

How could this scenario have been prevented and what was the impact of the process? Prevention comes down to board leadership—nothing more, nothing less.

The impact of the meeting left many board members disillusioned. That day, the board leadership lost credibility and it took considerable time to regain it.

How does this true story apply to your board and to your ministry? You may serve on boards for years and never be part of a major merger. But these principles, mode of meeting, and allocation of board time are overarching concepts for many board meetings.

Let's look at each of these principles.

- **Meeting Principle #1: Meeting mode.** There is often a temptation to use a conference call when an in-person meeting is required for appropriate communication among board members. This temptation is heightened when technology allows board members to see each other.

As a participant in many board conference calls, my conclusion is that conference calls—with video or with audio only—are rarely appropriate for anything other than sharing a report or minor decision-making. The more effective dynamics of an in-person board meeting are difficult to replicate online.

- **Meeting Principle #2: Meeting time allocation.** How can we allocate appropriate time on meeting agendas?

    ☐ **Board chair-ministry leader collaboration.** Sound allocation of meeting time generally happens only when the board chair and the ministry's leader work closely together. When the board chair and the ministry leader are one and the same, this can be a short conversation.

    ☐ **Discernment in allocating time.** The board chair and the ministry leader work closely together in allocating agenda time. Godly discernment is also necessary in determining how much time to set aside for the most significant issues.

    One of the keys is a time cushion. If a board agenda has some flex time built in, then when the board goes long in discussing one issue, the chair knows that the cushion can be used to keep the overall agenda on track.

    ☐ **Outstanding execution.** This is where the importance of the board chair shines brilliantly. Even when the board chair and ministry leader have designed a solid agenda with a time cushion built in, it often requires deft execution by the board chair to keep a meeting on track.

An unflappable board chair doesn't lose his or her cool when the meeting is running behind the time allocated. The board chair looks for opportunities to make up the time—perhaps shortening a recess, extending the meeting hours a little, and gently encouraging members to stay focused.

BOARDROOM LESSON

Don't be pressed for time!
Always make major decisions at an in-person board meeting.

Board Action Steps:

○ 1. **Discern:** Carefully consider whether issues, other than reports or basic procedural matters, should be included on conference call agendas.

○ 2. **Prioritize:** Allot adequate time for discussion and discernment of major agenda items.

○ 3. **Flex:** When an improper meeting mode has been chosen or inadequate time has been allocated for a major agenda item, be willing to make a course correction mid-meeting, if necessary.

Prayer
Lord, give us great wisdom in planning
and executing our board meetings.
Amen.

30 | ARE YOU COMPETING BASED ON OVERHEAD— REALLY?

Boards should know the back-story on a ministry's overhead.

Too often, boards have little understanding
of functional expense allocations
and how the ministry promotes the results of the allocations.

Picture this. As a board member, you notice that your ministry is proudly proclaiming that overhead expenses are only 12 percent. Prospective givers are told their gifts will have a greater impact—compared to their giving to other ministries.

But you wonder if that comparison is wise. So in the board-room, you gingerly ask the CEO, "I hope you don't think I'm in the operational weeds here, but has your team thought this through? Is our low overhead percentage really a key talking point in our fundraising story?"

At first glance, it may seem like an operational issue. However, the manner in which a ministry promotes itself is clearly a big picture issue—and big-picture issues are board issues.

Unfortunately, the giving public too often looks for one piece of data to inform them whether a ministry is worthy of their support and they have been led to believe that program expenses are good and fundraising and administrative expenses are bad. Moreover, they have also come to believe that the higher the good expenses are in relation to the bad expenses, the more efficient or effective a ministry is.

We've often noted, "In many cases, the difference between the overhead ratios of two very similar ministries is more a function of accounting methods than operational differences."[1] Effectiveness and efficiency are not functions of overhead allocations.

Ministries often promote their outcomes and impact—how God is using the ministry to fulfill its mission and further the Great Commission. Now that's something to promote—but not in a comparative way.

A ministry's overhead percentage is based on numbers on the financial statements, but it is not the

> *Effectiveness and efficiency are not functions of overhead allocations.*

type of information to be *promoted*. It is only information to be *reported*. To promote a ministry's overhead percentage suggests a level of precision that does not exist.

Some of a ministry's accounting information is hard data, such as cash in the bank and the mortgage balance. However, some of the largest elements of the accounting information are often soft, such as how much of compensation is allocated to overhead and how much is program expense.

Accounting rules only provide general guidelines on the allocation of expenses. The method of allocating the expenses simply must be reasonable and consistently applied. And "reasonableness" is in the eye of the ministry and its CPA firm.[2] As Michael Batts says, "Functional expense reporting is voodoo."[3]

So what should a board know about a ministry's overhead allocations?

1. **The overhead percentage.** A board should know the overhead percentages that are reported on the annual financial statements and to the IRS, if applicable.

2. **Inclusions in overhead and program expense.** A board should have a general idea of the types of expenses that are allocated to overhead vs. program.

3. **The ministry's philosophy in allocating overhead expenses.** Board members should understand how much emphasis is placed on overhead allocations. Does the CEO tell the accounting department that the goal is to report overhead of a specific percentage for the year? Or is the accounting department given the freedom to appropriately minimize overhead allocations without pressure to hit a certain target?

4. **How overhead data is communicated to the ministry's constituents.** Is the ministry measuring its performance based on subjective expense allocations? Is a low overhead number promoted as a reason why givers should support the ministry? Is the ministry's comparative rating by outside groups, with the ratings significantly based on overhead percentages, used to compete with other ministries?

What should a board do with this overhead knowledge? A board should be familiar and comfortable with the ministry's overall approach to handling overhead expenses. This includes the functional expense process and especially how this information is being shared with prospective givers.

BOARDROOM LESSON

Don't be tempted to raise funds inappropriately
by touting low overhead rates.
Overhead rates are highly subjective and defy precision.

Board Action Steps:

○ 1. **Educate:** Invest time in helping the board clearly understand the big picture of ministry overhead allocations.

○ 2. **Approve:** Once the board learns the basics of the ministry's philosophy of allocating overhead expenses, affirm the principles in the Board Policies Manual.

○ 3. **Communicate:** Ensure that the board is at an appropriate comfort level when communicating overhead expense information to constituents.

Prayer
Lord, help our ministry communicate our
performance with clarity and integrity using
sound concepts and principles.
Amen.

31 | WHERE TWO OR THREE ARE GATHERED ON SOCIAL MEDIA . . .

Conflicts of interest always sound more salacious on the internet and social media.

Boards often become convinced that they are making a decision in the best interest of the ministry. But they fail to consider how the decision would appear on the internet and social media.

Ministries purchase many services or products—from information technology to lawn service to facility maintenance, construction projects, and much more.

And when a ministry spends a significant amount of money with someone who is on the board or staff, or related to a board or staff member, the risk level goes up. Even if the transaction is in the best interest of the ministry, a perception of impropriety can easily arise.

For example, one ministry was in the initial planning stage of a multimillion-dollar capital campaign. Three consulting firms presented proposals to lead the campaign. One of the firms was owned by the son of one board member.

The consulting services offered by the three firms were comparable, and the proposal by the board member's son was the least expensive to the ministry, but it was still well over $100,000.

The ministry had a well-written conflicts of interest policy. The board's decision technically complied with their policy. They considered the three paths shown below and they approved a contract with the firm led by the son of a board member (Path 2). Later they wished they had turned down the contract out of an abundance of caution (Path 3).

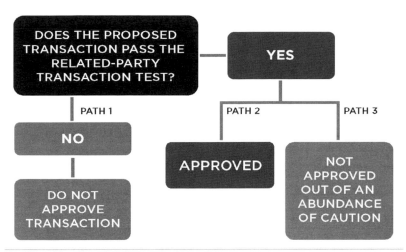

PATH 1:
DO NOT APPROVE!
If the transaction is not in the best interest of the ministry, it should not be approved because it would inappropriately elevate a competing interest over the ministry's fiduciary interest.

PATH 2:
APPROVED!
A significant related-party transaction could be approved after disclosing it to the ministry's governing board who, after recusing related parties, determines the transaction is advantageous to the ministry, with a commitment to make appropriate disclosures.

PATH 3:
NOT APPROVED!
The ministry could decide not to approve the related-party transaction, perhaps out of an abundance of caution if a significantly negative perception could surround the transaction.

The capital campaign began well, but after a couple of the lead gifts were unexpectedly withdrawn, meeting the campaign goal became doubtful. Twelve months later, the campaign quietly ended with only 30 percent of the goal met.

The recrimination began. Some major givers to the campaign asked for a refund of their gifts. Soon the attention turned to the quality of the campaign consulting firm and whether the firm was a good choice. Next, the failed campaign and the choice of the consultant found its way to social media.

> *While the board followed the proper steps in approving the transaction, they did not adequately consider how the transaction would be viewed—especially on the internet and social media.*

The facts about the campaign disappeared in the rearview mirror. Blog posts with many inaccurate assumptions about the campaign appeared. The major issue highlighted on the posts was the choice of the board member's son as the campaign consultant.

Social media threads became very nasty. Only a few of the comments were from campaign givers; most were from non-contributors who had never been involved in the ministry.

At this point, there were several decisions the board wished they had not made. At the top of the list: their choice of the consultant. Oh, for a mulligan on that decision! While the board followed the proper steps in approving the transaction, they did not adequately consider how the transaction could be viewed—especially on the internet and social media.

The ministry survived the botched capital campaign, but it was painful and expensive. The issue consumed many hours of the board's time, spanning two years of board meetings. A number of givers stopped supporting the ministry as a result of the campaign.

It was a lesson well-learned and a path they would not retrace—at least not until the current board members were off the board and new members filled their seats.

Moving forward, the board committed to carefully follow these four steps when considering significant transactions involving related parties:

1. **Exclude.** All individuals with a conflict of interest, direct or indirect, will be excluded from the discussion and the vote related to the transaction.

2. **Compare.** Reliable comparability information from appropriate independent sources will be considered, such as competitive bids, independent appraisals, or independent expert opinions.

3. **Determine.** It will be determined whether the transaction is in the overall best interest of the ministry, including determining whether the transaction could be misperceived by givers, constituents, or the public. *Remember, the transaction will likely be publicly disclosed.*

4. **Document.** Steps 1, 2, and 3 will be documented in a timely manner.

Even when the ministry takes those four essential steps, it may still be in the best interest of the ministry to avoid the related-party transaction.

You can be sure that many ministries would like to have a do-over on certain related-party transaction decisions they have made. Even when the ministry checked all the boxes, they did not consider how the transaction would be viewed—especially on the internet and social media.

BOARDROOM LESSON

When the boardroom doors are shut, transactions with related parties often take on a golden hue. When the same decision is subjected to the bright light of the internet, it can look starkly different.

Board Action Steps:

○ 1. **Discuss:** Review the ministry's conflict of interest policy for adequacy.

○ 2. **Determine:** Next, determine if the board consistently follows the conflict of interest policy.

○ 3. **Discern:** Ensure that the board considers the possible ministry impact if the related-party transaction is disclosed on the internet or social media. (For more resources, download *ECFA Governance Toolbox Series No. 3: Conflicts of Interest.*[1])

Prayer

Lord, help us to consider the long-range impact of every significant decision involving related parties. Amen.

PART 9:

HOLY GROUND
AND OTHER LOCATIONS

Let me not today embark on no undertaking
that is not in line with Thy will for my life,
nor shrink from any sacrifice
which Thy will may demand.[1]

John Baillie

32

THERE ARE TWO THINGS YOU SHOULD NEVER JOKE ABOUT— #1: PRAYER

"The last one with your thumb up says grace."

Those of us who deal in words are at great risk of misusing words and even sinning with words due to the sheer volume of them. I don't know about you, but sometimes I can literally feel— deep in my bones—that if I do not shut my mouth for a while I will get myself in trouble, because my words will be completely disconnected from the reality of God in my life.[1]

Ruth Haley Barton

Olan Hendrix, the founding president of ECFA, served in his fair share of ministry boardrooms across the country and around the world. Untold numbers of leaders, like John Maxwell, point to wisdom gleaned from Olan Hendrix for those critical fork-in-the-road decisions in their leadership journeys.[2]

We especially appreciate Olan's insights on an unusual topic: "Two Things You Should Never Joke About: Prayer and Fundraising." Both insights, if lived out in the boardroom, will enhance your board's understanding that wherever board members gather is holy ground. Discern together, as a board, how this wisdom from Olan adds another layer to the distinctiveness of Christ-centered governance.

During an informal session with emerging young leaders in 1999, Olan cautioned that there are some things you should never joke about. When one young leader asked for examples, he explained why prayer and fundraising should never be the subject of jokes. Later he wrote about it.

Olan Hendrix on Why You Should Never Joke About Prayer:

I couldn't believe my ears! My client, who had retained me to search for an individual to fill a key position in his organization, told me he was rejecting the candidate I had recommended. I was convinced the man met all the job qualifications. He had an impressive track record, and seemed ideal for the position. His life was in order, and he fit the doctrinal mold exactly.

Nevertheless, he was rejected—because it turned out he had made light of prayer. When my client learned this person had made a tasteless joke on the subject, he was disturbed enough to remove him from further consideration.

We need humor in our lives, but only humor that lifts the heart. Making light of the sacred can only be harmful.

Naturally, I accepted his decision, but was astonished that one single negative factor would outweigh the many positive ones.

That was many years ago and I no longer remember the joke, but I've never been able to forget the incident. My client was absolutely right.

While I've never considered prayer to be a joking matter, he helped me to begin to understand something of the solemnity of the believer communing with God.

Humor is not only a useful tool, it's also a valuable relief valve. Our spirits can be lifted in a moment of sadness by a funny story. A tense meeting can be spared a disruption by a bit of humor. We need humor in our lives, but only humor that lifts the heart. Making light of the sacred, no matter what our intentions, can only be harmful.[3]

Bob Kelly also observed in an issue of *CMA Management Monthly*, "It's not uncommon to be part of a group at mealtime and have one thoughtless companion joke, 'Last one with your thumb up says grace.'"[4]

Kelly then asked readers to contrast that flippant kind of disrespect for God, the Provider of all things, with this from Charles H. Spurgeon:

God does not hear us because of the length of our prayer, but because of the sincerity of it. Prayer is not to be measured by the yard, nor weighed by the pound. It is the might and force of it—the truth and reality of it—the energy and the intensity of it.[5]

Note: Read Lesson 33 to learn why Olan Hendrix says you should also never joke about fundraising.

BOARDROOM LESSON

There are two things you should never joke about—
and the first one is prayer. Is there a deep sense
during your board meetings (and when two or more board
members gather together) that you are on holy ground?
Do board members pray with solemnity—valuing the
immense privilege of communing with our Holy God?

Board Action Steps:

○ 1. **Pray:** From the beginning to the end of your board
meetings—and spontaneously as issues arise—create
a praying culture that demonstrates to all that your
boardroom is on holy ground.

○ 2. **Intercede:** Identify board members who have the
spiritual gift of intercessory prayer—and invite them
to leverage that gift in the boardroom.

○ 3. **Model:** Rather than a "last thumb up" approach that
trivializes prayer, use mealtimes with your board as an
opportunity to model intentionality about prayer and
gratitude.

Prayer
Lord, teach us to pray.
Amen.

33 THERE ARE TWO THINGS YOU SHOULD NEVER JOKE ABOUT— #2: FUNDRAISING

Flippancy about fundraising is never a
good substitute for sincerity.

Board members, are you committed personally
to this journey for yourselves, seeking to be faithful stewards
whose hearts are rich toward God?
You are the model for your communities. Generosity in giving
to your organization starts with you. Others will support your work
as they see you giving generously and joyfully.[1]

R. Scott Rodin

During an informal session with emerging young leaders,
Olan Hendrix, the founding president of ECFA, cautioned
that there are some things you should never joke about.

Board members, and often new board members, bring into
the boardroom a wide range of views and opinions about
fundraising and generosity, and frequently those beliefs are
not biblical. Plus, not all board members are effective
fundraisers. That sometimes skews them toward an unhealthy
fundraising approach or board policy.

Sometimes a board member's inferiority complex, or lack of
experience—or bad experience—about fundraising prompts

your board to default to inappropriate or even unbiblical practices. So heed this wisdom from Olan Hendrix.

Olan Hendrix on Why You Should Never Joke About Fundraising:

The raising of money is very serious business—very serious ministry—and we must treat it so.

I once accompanied a client on a donor call. This Christian leader had a worthwhile cause and many friends, but wasn't raising any money. I wanted to find out why.

After exchanging pleasantries with the donor, he began making jokes about the fact that he was there to ask for money. I had discovered his problem! Perhaps he was covering up his nervousness about asking for money, but flippancy is never a good substitute for sincerity.

> *Perhaps he was covering up his nervousness about asking for money, but flippancy is never a good substitute for sincerity.*

God's own design for advancing the Kingdom includes the proper asking of funds. We never apologize for the Gospel or the Ten Commandments—nor should we apologize when we ask believers to be generous with their financial resources.

Fundraising is ministry, even though the world generally sees it as begging. We often adopt that thinking to our detriment. I want a part of my legacy to be that I helped God's servants to see fundraising not as something to joke about or apologize for, but as a noble and vital part of ministry.[2]

If your board members need training and encouragement in generosity and fundraising, give them the short novelette by R. Scott Rodin, *The Third Conversion*. He quotes Martin Luther: "There are three conversions necessary to every man; the head, the heart and the purse."[3] Rodin adds this on creating a culture of giving:

> Organizations as well as individuals are embarked on a journey of faith and faithfulness. For an organization, this journey is influenced primarily by its culture. And ministry leaders are culture keepers. They are tasked to define reality, articulate values, and exhibit consistent behaviors that become the cultural moorings of the organization. When organizations define their reality in kingdom terms, articulate their values in alignment with biblical, holistic stewardship, and exhibit behaviors that indicate their commitment to the journey of the faithful steward, they engender a culture of giving.[4]

BOARDROOM LESSON

Not every board member is a skilled fundraiser—
and that's okay. Yet every board member can hold high
the serious ministry of raising Kingdom resources.
Is fundraising, like prayer, treated with importance
and seriousness in your boardroom?
Are your values in alignment with biblical values
on generosity and stewardship?

Board Action Steps:

○ 1. **Read:** Ask a board member to read and report on *The Third Conversion* by R. Scott Rodin.

○ 2. **Study:** To compare your values against Kingdom values, study *The Sower: Redefining the Ministry of Raising Kingdom Resources* by R. Scott Rodin and Gary G. Hoag.[5]

○ 3. **Equip:** According to *Unleashing Your Board's Potential: Comprehensive Report from ECFA's Nonprofit Governance Survey*, although 86 percent of boards expect board members to encourage others to give, less than 32 percent of those organizations have equipped and trained board members in fundraising.[6]

Prayer
Lord, don't let my perceived lack of confidence in
fundraising get in the way of the biblical generosity
journey You want me to share with others.
Amen.

34 | FIVE TROUBLESOME MISCONCEPTIONS OF BOARD MEMBERS

Understanding board member myths can lead to improved governing effectiveness.

Many misconceptions of board members can be eliminated through healthy dialogue and early education.

Some individuals join ministry boards thinking their responsibilities will be an easy task. *What a misconception!* And in many cases, the larger the ministry, the more challenging the board service. This work is only for committed, serious-minded followers of Christ.

Identifying and overcoming misconceptions through board education is an important and ongoing process. Here are five governance misconceptions that should be addressed:

- **Misconception #1.** *Board members know exactly what to do once they are elected to the board.*

  Many new board members take their seat with little or no ministry board experience. In fact, they may have little board experience of any kind. ECFA research says that one in five boards need "much" or "major" help in better orienting new board members.[1] If their board experience was on the board of a large for-profit corporation, the board may have only met twice a year compared to the more frequent meetings of many ministries.

Board members often express frustration over the CEO's expectations. As Michael Anthony says, "It was as if the day they were elected to the board, the [CEO] assumed that a mantle of wisdom and discernment came magically on them from on high."[2]

Little or no board experience heightens the importance of board training. Unfortunately, training rarely occurs for ministry board members. They are expected to be "trained on the job."

Larry Osborne writes, "Frustrated with our inability to find time to deal with these vital issues, I hit on an idea. "Why not schedule an extra monthly meeting to deal exclusively with (1) team building, (2) training, and (3) prayer."[3]

- **Misconception #2.** *Board members have a great deal of free time.*

The best board members are almost always the busiest of people. If CEOs fail to recognize the often frenzied lives of board members, they do so at their own peril.

Especially if both spouses work and there are children living at home, it is challenging to find time for frequent board meetings, let alone the additional board meetings called perhaps with little notice.

One possible solution to avoiding burnout of board members is to adopt a policy that board members do not serve in any other capacity in the ministry. While there is the temptation to also direct an outreach event, it is usually best for board members to focus their energies on their highest calling at the ministry—the board.

- **Misconception #3.** *Most board members have a basic understanding of nonprofit finances, including fundamental tax issues.*

  Even board members who have served on a ministry board for years may find it challenging to comprehend financial data. There are several reasons for this:

  - Nonprofit financial data is rarely presented to the board in comprehensible form. This is often not the fault of the staff or volunteers who have financial reporting responsibilities. Computer software available for nonprofits often limits meaningful communication of the data.

  - Savvy financial statement readers must master the concepts of accounting methods (accrual, modified cash, and cash), expensing or capitalizing property and equipment, depreciation of property and equipment, reporting restricted (designated) gifts, and much more.

- ❏ **Misconception #4.** *Nonprofits are simple entities and they are easily understood by board members.*

  Nothing could be further from the truth. Even smaller ministries find themselves slogging along in a swamp of regulations, tax filings, legal issues and more.

  Ministries face a landscape filled with payroll tax filings even if they have just one employee. Then there are filings for independent contractors. Some ministries must also file unrelated business income tax returns.

No, nonprofits are not simple entities. Serving on a governing board at a nonprofit ministry is not for the weak at heart.

- **Misconception #5.** *It is easy for ministry boards to avoid micromanaging.*

Steve Stroope says, "One of the key dangers for boards is the temptation to micromanage, which does not allow staff leaders to do their jobs or execute the responsibilities for which they were hired. Micromanaging boards come about partially due to the fact that [board members] have not been properly trained in regards to their roles."[4] At Lake Pointe Church in Houston, where Steve pastored for many years, elders are given a detailed policy about the board and its relationship to the pastor.

Boards must say no to most issues that could create agenda clutter. Simply because the CEO or a board member proposes an agenda item does not mean the board should discuss it. While saying no to agenda items is not easy, the health of the board, and perhaps the ministry, is at stake.[4]

Avoiding micromanagement may be a ministry board's biggest challenge. Why is this? Probably because board members are so close to the action. It is so easy to be hands on since board members are often very familiar with some of the detailed operations of the ministry.

Identifying and understanding boardroom misconceptions will enable your board to improve its effectiveness. It's worth the effort!

BOARDROOM LESSON

Understand the key misconceptions about
board members and board service.
How effectively the ministry deals with these misconceptions
will greatly determine the impact of the board.

Board Action Steps:

○ 1. **Identify:** Identify what misconceptions might exist concerning your board members and their board service.

○ 2. **Confirm:** Confirm which misconceptions really exist by discussing common misconceptions with the board or by taking an informal poll of board members regarding their perceptions of board service.

○ 3. **Go to Work:** Take appropriate steps to address each misconception. Educate the board until all misconceptions are eliminated.

Prayer
Lord, thank You for every board member
and the time each person invests in this holy calling.
Give us courage—and grace—to address
misconceptions that can diminish our effectiveness.
Amen.

35 | LEVERAGE THE 80/20 RULE IN THE BOARDROOM

Invest 80 percent of your board work on future ministry opportunities—not rehashing the past.

Effective executives, in my observation, do not start with their tasks. They start with their time. And they do not start out with planning. They start by finding out where their time actually goes.[1]

Peter F. Drucker

A board governance colleague, Gordon Flinn, introduced us to the brilliant concept of the 80/20 Rule in the Boardroom. Here's the big idea:

If your CEO and board chair do not proactively create a forward-looking board meeting agenda, you'll squander the board's time. And worse— you'll squander those ministry opportunities that have eternal consequences. Focus on the future. Inspire your board members to be discerning where God wants you to minister—because as Henry Blackaby notes, "God reveals His will and invites you to join Him where He is already at work."[2]

POP QUIZ!

Which board meeting agenda will inspire and engage board members to bring their best into your boardroom?

☑ CHECK ONE:

❑ **Dead Sea Ministries Monthly Board Meeting Agenda**	❑ **Mega Impact Ministries Quarterly Board Meeting Agenda**
• Call to Order • Prayer • Minutes • Committee Reports • More Committee Reports • Old Business • Really Old Business • New Business (if there's time!) • Prayer • Adjournment	• Welcome & Refreshments • Prayer in Small Groups • 10 Minutes for Governance[3] • **Heavy Lifting Topic:** "Drucker Question #3: What Does Our Customer Value?"[4] (60 min.) • Recommendations from Committees • Consent Agenda (including approval of board minutes) • **80/20 Rule Recommendations:** (80% focused on our future) • Next Steps and Accountability • Five-Finger Feedback[5] • Doxology

We know. We know. It's so tempting for some board members to obsess ad nauseam over last quarter's numbers. Others will micromanage down in the weeds and interject irrelevant topics unrelated to Kingdom advancement. Still others will inappropriately wear their volunteer hats in the boardroom. But for the sake of the ministry, you must inspire board members to resist these temptations. (Encourage them to read Lesson 26: "Big Rocks, Pebbles, and Sand.")

We've seen dozens of boards who major on the minors, and minor on the majors. *But good news—there is a solution.* If your board recently squandered an hour rehashing mistakes of the past—rather than creating best practice policies to give you guardrails for the future—talk about this ministry-changing "80/20 Rule." (You may be familiar with Vilfredo Pareto's 80/20 rule, but this is a new application of that rule).[6]

The best boards, we believe, have a very strategic 80/20 rule:

- Great boards invest 80% of board work on the future.

- And great boards allocate only 20% of board work on the past.

That sounds easy—but just review the minutes of your last four board meetings. It's quite possible your board has reversed the ratio:

- Investing just 20% of board time on the future.

- Allocating 80% of board time on rehashing the past.

In fact, one of ECFA's research projects asked nonprofit board members, "Roughly what percent of a typical board meeting is spent on the FUTURE (as opposed to reviewing the present or past)?" Only 49 percent said that they spend half or more of their meeting on the future. Interestingly, CEO's responses were a bit lower than 49 percent and board member responses were a bit higher, meaning that CEOs don't sense a "future focus" as strongly as board members do.

> *Great boards invest time on their knees to discern direction.*

We then divided the survey responders into two groups: those who agreed that their board is effective and those who didn't. Among boards that rate themselves as effective, 87 percent spend half or more of a typical meeting dealing with the future.[7]

You must avoid *Rearview Mirror Syndrome*! For a tool to help you focus on the future, consider using a strategy map process—a graphic representation of the "resources, processes, and product/service offerings necessary to achieve your goals."[8]

According to George Babbes and Michael Zigarelli, one benefit of the strategy map is that this process will move "your ministry past the traditional focus on lagging indicators, such as [program participation] and [donor giving] (indicators that essentially tell you about your past performance), and on to leading indicators, such as innovative programs in the pipeline, member satisfaction, and available staff and volunteer talent (indicators that tell you where you're headed in the future).

> Stated differently, an exclusive focus on outcomes such as membership or financial health is like looking in a rearview mirror: they only tell you where you've been. In contrast, a focus on things such as the number of new discipleship initiatives ready for introduction or the spiritual maturity of your members foreshadow what's likely to occur spiritually and financially for months or even years to come. In this way, a strategy map is an indispensable tool for any ministry to "excel still more" (1 Thessalonians 4:1 NASB).[9]

And yes, we have anticipated your next question. "But . . . I'm not sure our board would know what to do if we allocated 80 percent of our board meeting time on the future!"

There are many ways to inspire your board to be future-focused. Here are six ideas:

☑ **Great boards** allocate a two-hour or three-hour block, quarterly, for heavy lifting or big rocks. This might include pre-reading assignments and a task force's major analysis of a critical topic, such as "Turning the Flywheel" and this question: "What are the four to six components that are unique to our ministry's flywheel?" (Read the 40-page booklet by Jim Collins.)[10]

☑ **Great boards** have a robust strategic planning process. Some use a *Rolling 3-Year Strategic Plan* approach with a one-page document summarizing three to five initiatives—with annual benchmarks over three years.[11] The one-pager is updated annually like clockwork—similar to the budgeting process.

☑ **Great boards** engage the board and senior team members in trend-spotting year-round but especially at the board's annual planning retreat. Some boards use a trend-spotting exercise that invites every board member to research and report on relevant trends.[12]

☑ **Great boards** "own the strategy"[13] to ensure new programs, products, and services are in alignment with a staff-prepared and board-approved two-page summary of the ministry's strategy (a critical component of the strategic planning process).

☑ **Great boards** appoint a "Readers Are Leaders"[14] champion—a book zealot who inspires the board to read and discuss at least one future-focused book each year.[15]

☑ **Great boards** invest time on their knees to discern direction. They are mindful of Ruth Haley Barton's wisdom, "Just because something is strategic does not necessarily mean it is God's will for us right now."[16] Prolonged periods of prayer should translate into more time to discern God's plans for the future—instead of more time devoted to *confession* for the ministry's sins of the past!

Gordon Flinn, our trend-spotter on the "80/20 Rule" noted that Peter Drucker, the father of modern management, said that systematic innovation (always looking ahead) includes leveraging seven sources for innovative opportunity. Drucker said to watch for three changes outside of your organization, including 1) demographics, 2) changes in perception, mood, and meaning, and 3) new knowledge.[17] That's a meaty future-focused topic for your next "heavy lifting" session!

The Apostle Paul wrote, "Be very careful, then, how you live—not as unwise but as wise, making the most of every opportunity, because the days are evil. Therefore do not be foolish, but understand what the Lord's will is" (Ephesians 5:15-17, NIV).

This is challenging work for any board—and to land on God-honoring priorities and direction takes time. But if you squander 80 percent of your board time analyzing the past, the remaining 20 percent will be sorely inadequate for fully discussing and discerning God's plan for your ministry in this needy world.

BOARDROOM LESSON

Redeem the time in every board meeting.
Establish priorities and policies that will give guidance
to the allocation of resources and the fulfillment of God's
mission for your ministry. Invest 80 percent of your
board meeting time looking forward, not looking back.

Board Action Steps:

○ **1. Search:** Review recent board minutes to assess if your
board is investing 80 percent of your valuable time on
looking forward.

○ **2. Stop:** If an inappropriate amount of time is spent
looking back—stop! Refresh your agenda (see Lesson
26) so you focus on heavy lifting and big rocks and
board-level policies and priorities.

Prayer
Lord, as Psalm 90:12 reminds us,
"Teach us to number our days,
that we may gain a heart of wisdom."
Amen.

PART 10:

BUILDING A 24/7
BOARD CULTURE

You must be diligent as a director.
Make sure that you ask any questions that are on your mind.
As the saying goes, the only bad question is
the one you had but didn't ask.[1]

John Pellowe

36

WATCH OUT FOR BOARDS ASLEEP AT THE WHEEL

Golden opportunities are missed when a board's eyes are wide shut.

The drone of routine board meetings often creates un-memorable results.

It was a Busby family vacation trip to Texas. It was a very hot summer day. The road was long and straight. Our two children were asleep in the back seat. My wife was asleep in the front. The car was on cruise control. *And I was tired.*

There are the times when your eyelids get heavy and you fight off drowsiness. This was not one of those times. This was full-blown, eyes entirely shut, asleep.

I didn't feel a thing when the car edged off of the interstate and into the wide ditch. I woke up to the swishing of tall grass hitting the front bumper and windows as we plowed a 70 mph path through the ditch.

Now, wide awake, I gently steered the car up the side of the ditch and back onto the interstate. I breathed a prayer of thanksgiving, and we continued our trek.

Likewise, boards can become drowsy and listless by slipping into a routine of grinding through yet another meeting. Here are four examples:

1. **Improper use of restricted gifts.**[1] It is not unusual for a ministry to receive gifts restricted for a certain purpose (for example, child sponsorship, clean water projects, and so on) and then borrow the funds for operational purposes. Worse yet is when a ministry expends restricted gifts for a purpose inconsistent with the giver's restriction, with no plans to replace the money into the restricted account. *Asleep at the wheel.*

2. **Disappearing reserves.** Many a ministry has gradually moved from a financially sound position to a troubled financial situation. This transition happened while board members routinely approved the budget and the annual financial reports.[2] Just one example: The budget was balanced, but significant resources were expended on capitalized items. *Asleep at the wheel.*

   > *The classic board that is asleep at the wheel is the board that spends too much of its time on operational matters.*

3. **Approving related-party transactions that are inappropriate.** Some transactions seem to be in the best interest of the ministry. Yet the close relationship of those involved and the significant dollar size of the transactions leaves observers convinced that the related-party dealings were inappropriate.[3] *Asleep at the wheel.* (Also, see Lesson 31.)

4. **Approve unreasonable operating budgets.** Every ministry should have a reasonable operating (and perhaps a capital expense) budget that is annually approved by the appropriate oversight body (e.g., board or committee).

The ministry budget provides a rail or a curb for influencing financial activity. It is important that the budget process supports the ministry's strategic plan. Unreasonable projections of revenue and expenses mean the ministry has adopted a stretch goal, which is almost impossible to attain. *Asleep at the wheel.*

5. **Leadership failure.** Sometimes a board will overlook or even miss the continuing chaos created by their CEO. When there is frequent turnover of board members, the

> *It is difficult to be focused and fully engaged when texting, tweeting, and responding to emails while the meeting is in progress.*

fact that the CEO has gone off the rails is often masked. *Asleep at the wheel.*

Boards most often fall asleep at that wheel when they:

- **Misread the landscape.** Acute discernment is necessary to sense what may be coming just around the corner. Without these keen insights into the future, a ministry may be too mired in the past to adjust to a rapidly changing climate.

- **Can't see the forest for the trees.** Having sound policies and following them is good. But some boards are so focused on policies that they fail to ask the insightful questions about the direction of the ministry. They have checked all the boxes (the trees) and missed the big picture (the forest).

- **Become mired in the weeds.** The classic board that is asleep at the wheel is the one that spends too much of its time on operational matters. This not only diminishes the role of the CEO but also makes it nearly impossible for the board to focus on the big picture.

Is your board asleep at the wheel? Remember that golden opportunities for Kingdom impact are missed when a board's eyes are wide shut.

BOARDROOM LESSON

Through commitment, dedication, and a focus on the big picture, boards can fight off mental drowsiness.

Board Action Steps:

○ 1. **Measure:** Review the board's recent history. Were we alert to the most important issues?

○ 2. **Create:** Invest energy, prayer, and creativity to plan board meetings that will be engaging and fulfilling for ministry leaders and board members.

○ 3. **Prioritize:** Ensure that board agendas address key issues requiring the board's generative thinking (see Lesson 2) and the board's heavy lifting.

Prayer
Lord, help our board to be fully present
in each board meeting, to maximize our time,
and to not be asleep at the wheel.
Amen.

37 | HOW MANY BOARD MEMBERS ARE PRESENT IN YOUR BOARDROOM?

It's more than just answering the roll call.

The technology we carry with us into board meetings significantly contributes to Board Attention Deficit Disorder (BADD).

When all board members are assembled in the boardroom for a board meeting—well, at least the ones who arrived on time—there is the usual friendly chatter (that is a *good* sign). It generally takes a few minutes before the members get quiet and are ready for the call of the roll.

When a board member says "present" or "here," what does that really mean? Sometimes, it means he or she is merely physically in the boardroom.

Board members are some of the busiest people we know. They probably wouldn't be good board members if people were not clamoring for their time, their wisdom, and their leadership.

The down side is that busy people often have a hard time tuning *out* their busy lives and tuning *in* to the work of the board. Most of them find it especially challenging to turn off their technology and be truly present in the boardroom.

You have probably seen this picture. One board member is working on her computer writing an overdue report—another on his tablet answering emails or working on personal projects while feigning attention to the discussion around the boardroom table.

Another common scenario is when board members attempt to conceal a hand-held device below the boardroom table while texting or emailing.

The result? Board members are physically in the room but they are not truly present. Total presence of each board member is necessary to conduct board business at a high level. Otherwise, a board is just going through the motions— just "phoning it in."

At the outset of a recent board meeting, the board chair stated that the meeting agenda included issues requiring heavy lifting. He challenged the board to be highly focused and avoid being interrupted by their technology. He said, "My laptop is in my briefcase. I am turning off my phone and placing it on the table. I challenge each of you to do the same."

The downside is that busy people often have a hard time tuning out their busy lives and tuning in to the work of the board. Most of them find it especially challenging to turn off their technology and be truly present in the boardroom.

While the board chair's statements may have caused some of the board members to take a deep breath, one by one each board member turned off their devices. What followed was one of the board's most highly engaged and productive meetings.

Can board members discern and discuss important issues and clearly hear from the Holy Spirit while multitasking with their technology during a board meeting? *We doubt it.*

Going AWOL on the board meeting "presence" scale is not just about technological interruptions. There are also factors unrelated to technology that cause board members to tune out. Here are a few of these causes:

- **Board meetings that are held too frequently.** Some ministry boards meet whether there is a solid agenda for a meeting or not. Weak agendas cause wandering minds in the boardroom. Without a strong monthly agenda, consider meeting less frequently to increase boardroom focus and productivity.

- **Meetings that run too long.** Few things will kill the attention of board members like a meeting that seems to continue into eternity. One of the ministry boards which I served on for nearly 20 years had multi-day meetings, including meetings in the evenings. As an evening meeting wore on, the board chair would monitor board attentiveness and the clock. When the clock struck 9 p.m., he would often say "Unless we adjourn for the evening, we will be presuming on the grace of God." And, he was so right! Better would have been to plan shorter meeting times to ensure the board's maximum attention for the duration of the meeting.

- **Board meetings conducted in a physical location not conducive to focused board work.** Few boards can meet in a tranquil, mind-clearing location with a view of Pike's Peak or of the ocean. But most boards can and should meet in surroundings that are well-lit, appropriately decorated, and with adequate space. These factors will improve attentiveness.

Whether it is avoiding technological interruptions or addressing other issues that detract from a focused board meeting, finding a way to maximize the total presence of all board members is vital.

BOARDROOM LESSON

Minimizing boardroom distractions will maximize meeting impact and enhance the possibility of hearing the still, small voice of the Holy Spirit.

Board Action Steps:

○ 1. **Assess:** Are all of your board members really present in each board meeting? If not, is it just one or two board members who are consistently distracted or is it a general condition of the board? Which distractions are the most serious in nature?

○ 2. **Evaluate:** If distractions, especially from technology, are prevalent, how can the condition best be addressed by the board chair?

○ 3. **Develop:** Create an action plan to determine which issues need to be addressed "full throttle" and perhaps decide on other issues which can be alleviated with some gentle reminders.

Prayer
Lord, help our board to be truly present,
in every sense of the word, during our board meetings.
Amen.

38 | SEVEN TIMES WHEN A BOARD MEMBER SHOULD BID ADIEU

Board service is for a season—but it is not forever!

Wise people know when to quit.[1]

Dr. Henry Cloud

Board service is some of the most rewarding work that you can ever do. And nearly every individual joins a board with hopes and dreams to make a difference. But even in the best of board service situations—it is not forever. And this is true even if the board on which you serve has no term limits.

Board members generally finish their terms with a sense of accomplishment. Some even lament when the time comes to leave a board. But there are times when a board member should leave a board—even mid-term.

While there are many situations when a board member should simply make a graceful exit from a board, we will only focus on seven of these opportunities:

1. **Your passion for the board work has waned.** When your passion to serve on the board has left the building, it is time to step off the board. Indicators of loss of passion are lack of faithful board meeting attendance, failure to prepare for board meetings, inattention during board meetings, and more.

If you are on a board with no term limits, the loss of passion could relate to how many years you have served on the board or perhaps your age. Or, board members can lose their passion by becoming too busy with other priorities to effectively serve.

Remember, *no passion equals low board service. Low board service equals board room doldrums.*

2. **You joined the board for the wrong reason.** If you joined a ministry board with the thought of expanding or increasing your business or building your resumé (see Lesson 18), you are not the first board member to do so. Perhaps you simply thought it would be prestigious to be a member of a certain ministry board.

> *No passion equals low board service. Low board service equals boardroom doldrums.*

Joining the board for the wrong reason is one thing—staying on a board after you realize that your motives were improper is something else. Quickly find an exit ramp!

3. **You determine that the board significantly lacks independence.** Once upon life's way, I accepted the invitation to join a certain national board of a significant ministry. I was enthusiastic about the opportunity to serve.

After a couple of meetings, it became obvious to me that I did not fit on the board. My first clue was that board meetings were only scheduled about 60 days in advance. Then I discerned that the board was comprised of the president/founder of the ministry and several of his "cronies." Along with the president's friends, I was just expected to rubber stamp his recommendations. They really didn't want my input—they were just borrowing my name and influence. I waited a year—should have waited less—and bid them goodbye. It was a decision I have never regretted.

4. **You have significant potential conflicts of interest.** When you began your board service, you did not have any relationships that were a potential conflict relating to your board service. But now, the ministry is investing several millions of dollars through the investment firm where you are a broker.

You were recused from the meeting when the board approved using your firm—plus the brokerage fees were competitive. (Also see Lesson 31). Another broker is handling the account and you do not receive any direct benefit from the account. But your brokerage firm clearly benefits from the relationship.

While the board is not bringing pressure on you to resign, in today's social media world, it would be easy for your ministry to be criticized for the decision to your brokerage firm. A resignation of your board membership is probably the better part of valor.

5. **The ministry is not conscientious about obeying the law.** The CEO and the ministry leadership team are comfortable with the legal compliance issues. Still it is clear that the ministry is not providing adequate accountability for funds expended internationally.

Representatives of the ministry are carrying cash of over $10,000 per trip out of the U.S. to provide funding for certain fields while not reporting the movement of the cash, the ministry had not met the charitable solicitation registration requirements in any of the applicable states.

You have politely raised concerns about the legal compliance in the last two meetings but none of the other board members share your concern. And the CEO and leadership team do not believe there is an issue. Their approach is "Let's wait to see if we get caught and then we will fix it."

In a last effort to highlight your concerns, you have a meeting with the board chair and the ministry's president. Still sensing there is not a heart to do what is right—and legal—you politely resign and wish them God's best.

6. **Not rowing in the same direction.** Vigorous debate is a mark of a strong board. Even seasoned ministry board members do not always agree with one another. However, after the debate is over and a decision has been made, everyone must row in the same direction—this means speaking with one voice.

   Once in a while a particular board member will be unable to support a decision made by the majority of the board members. This is a signal that it is time for the out-of-sync member to step off the board.

   Not rowing in the same direction often results in a board member feeling he or she doesn't have an effective voice:

- **Direction of the ministry.** It may become patently obvious to a board member that the ministry is headed in a strategic direction that the board member cannot support.

- **Conflicts between board members.** Friction between one board member and another board member can take all of the fun out of serving on a board—even if you aren't personally in the line of fire.

- **Conflicts between a board member and the CEO.** Sometimes there is such a fundamental divide between a board member and the CEO that board service becomes untenable.

> *After the debate is over and a decision has been made, everyone must row in the same direction.*

If you are serving as the lone dissenting board member—dissenting about the ministry's direction—or in conflict with other board members or the CEO, your service has effectively ended. Take the right step and resign.

7. **The ministry is in dire financial straits.** When a ministry is not doing well financially, board members can feel various levels of dis-ease. No board member wants to have their name associated with a ministry that is going under.

There is a big difference between a "financial rough spot" and dire financial straits:

- Financial hard times could be a run of several years of unrestricted expenses over revenue but the ministry still has some cash reserves—although the reserves are becoming more modest.

- Dire financial straits might be when the "B" word is mentioned—bankruptcy.

  Dire financial straits may lead to the ministry being no longer willing or able to provide Directors' and Officers' (D&O) liability insurance coverage for board members—most directors do not want to continue serving if the ministry is no longer able to provide the protection board members expect.

During financial hard times, board members, with God's help, *look for ways to get finances back on track*—by either increasing revenue or reducing expenses, or both. During a time of dire financial straits, board members often *look for the door.*

Before offering a formal resignation, raise your concerns to the board chair. It's possible that the rest of the board isn't aware of the concerns. Perhaps other board members may have some of the same concerns and your voicing them at the time of your resignation may bring those concerns out in the open, providing an opportunity for the board to discuss and resolve them.

BOARDROOM LESSON

Board service is for a season—but it is not forever!
A board chair should help board members determine
when their season of service is reaching an end

Board Action Steps:

○ 1. **Review:** At least annually, each board member should self-assess their board service.

○ 2. **Determine:** On a scale of 1-10 (10 is high), what is my passion for continued board service?

○ 3. **Take Action:** If my passion is waning for board service, is it time to consider stepping off the board? Learn why Dr. Henry Cloud writes, "Wise people know when to quit." Read *Necessary Endings: The Employees, Businesses, and Relationships That All of Us Have to Give Up in Order to Move Forward* by Dr. Henry Cloud (New York: HarperBusiness, 2010).

Prayer
Lord, help me discern when my time on the board
is over. Allow me to finish my service well.
Amen.

39 | IDENTIFY YOUR KEY ASSUMPTIONS

An inaccurate premise may lead to a colossal flop!

Meetings are a good place to discover whether an organization might be suffering from groupthink. If everyone in the room seems convinced of the brilliance of an idea, it may be a sign that the organization would benefit from more dissent and debate.[1]

Donald Rumsfeld

The silence was deafening. Board members gulped. Their red-in-the-face CEO had just delivered the shocking news. The *Vision 100 Challenge*—unanimously and enthusiastically affirmed by the board—had flopped.

Three major donors and a generous foundation had shared the ministry's enthusiasm for this out-of-the-box initiative. The largest donations in the organization's history were the sent-from-heaven lead gifts that fueled a robust fundraising campaign. *For the first time ever—lack of funds was not the problem.*

But there was a problem. The program—an enormously costly venture—had failed miserably.

Remember the story of the dog food company's annual sales meeting—when the VP of sales castigated her regional sales reps for declining sales? The executive harangued the discouraged sales agents: "What's going on here? We have the greatest ad campaigns. Our packaging is award-winning. We've improved distribution. So why are our dog food sales so dismal?"

An anonymous voice from the back of the room answered, **"The dogs don't like it!"**

Good news. There is help for dog food purveyors and ministry board members. At your next board meeting—ask this simple question:

"What are our assumptions about the _____?"

Just fill in the blanks with your current opportunity, project, or plan (strategic plan, annual plan, ABC Vision Initiative, XYZ Challenge, etc.).

Assumptions are a very big deal—and had the ministry above invested adequate time in identifying and elevating their key assumptions about the Vision 100 Challenge, they likely could have prevented an embarrassing flop and an egregious waste of God's money.

In the chapter "Thinking Strategically," in *Rumsfeld's Rules: Leadership Lessons in Business, Politics, War, and Life*, Donald Rumsfeld lists four critical strategic planning steps:

- Step 1: Set the Goals
- **Step 2: Identify Your Key Assumptions**

- Step 3: Determine the Best Course of Action

- Step 4: Monitor Progress Through Metrics[2]

Rumsfeld writes that the second step "tends to be one of the most neglected. Assumptions are often left unstated, it being taken for granted that everyone around a table knows what they are, when frequently that is not the case. The assumptions that are hidden or held subconsciously are the ones that often get you into trouble." (Think dog food—will the dogs like it?) He adds:

Had the ministry invested adequate time in identifying their key assumptions, they likely could have prevented an embarrassing flop and an egregious waste of God's money.

> It is possible to proceed perfectly logically from an inaccurate premise to an inaccurate and unfortunate conclusion.[3]

Rumsfeld, who was U.S. Secretary of Defense twice (and a Fortune 500 CEO twice), describes a planning meeting at the Pentagon: "The objective of the plan was straightforward enough: to defend South Korean sovereignty and defeat the North Korean threat. What I found troubling, however, was that there was no discussion of the key assumptions in which the plan was rooted."[4]

Rumsfeld dismissed the meeting and they reconvened on the next Saturday. "That Saturday we met for hours and never discussed any of the plans, only the assumptions."[5]

Are you willing to risk your ministry's future—with inadequate premises that lead to unfortunate conclusions?

We recommend you identify your "Top-10 Assumptions" that you believe are foundational to your programs, products, and services. Here are some well-assessed assumptions:

❑ **A rescue mission.** A social services ministry in a major city noted a trend that many of their homeless guests had previously lived in three nearby suburbs. *Assumption: If we create partnerships with key churches in key suburbs—and provide church leaders and volunteers with training and know-how—perhaps those churches could minister to local people in need before they are at a crisis point in their lives.*

❑ **A college.** The growing backlash against high tuition costs at private colleges may endanger the very existence of our Christian college (and even the need for a higher education). *Assumption: Within X years, student debt for graduating seniors must equate more to car loan levels versus home mortgage levels.*

❑ **A founder-led mission.** The aging donor base—hundreds and hundreds of faithful friends of the founder—will soon dry up as they pass on. *Assumption: Our future depends on our ability to inspire the children and grandchildren of our current donors to take the giving baton—before our founder retires (or dies).*

❑ **A media ministry.** The trends away from traditional TV and radio programming—toward podcasts and streaming—are the hot topics at our industry gatherings. *Assumption: We must break out of our traditional ministry model bubble (talking to ourselves, working harder—not smarter, etc.) and probably double our research budget immediately—so we're not caught flat-footed in a changing technological environment.*

Many boards and senior teams have intentional, robust discussions about assumptions—culminating in a one-page document (some call it their Radar Report). Then board members, the CEO, and senior team members look for opportunities to review that one-page report with stakeholders and trend-spotters—asking for informal feedback, like this:

> Mary, thanks for meeting with us today. In addition to talking about our capital campaign—would you look over this one-page list of "Our Top-10 Assumptions: The Radar Report" right now? Are these the right assumptions? What's missing? What would you add or delete?

We urge board members to be receptive to the Lord's "Tap! Tap! Tap!" on the shoulders of their hearts—not just at board meetings, but 24/7—every day.[6] Listen for the Holy Spirit's nudge—every day—and look for opportunities to discuss these assumptions with a colleague or even an acquaintance that is not familiar with your ministry. Perhaps God will plant just the right person in your path so your inaccurate assumptions don't lead to inaccurate conclusions—or a colossal flop!

There are many reasons why you should ask volunteers, donors, and others for feedback. R. Mark Dillon notes that "big ideas attract big gifts." He urges CEOs, pastors, and fundraisers to engage givers at the front end of a project. "Big ideas are mission-centered." He quotes one gifted giver, "Please don't come to me with an 'order list' already thought out, where my only decision is how much to give!"[7]

Dillon notes, "When the organization has done all the thinking and only wants capital from the giver, they have forfeited not only wise counsel but also a deeper relationship and, most probably the big gift as well."[8]

Rumsfeld would agree with Dillon. Here's a Rumsfeld rule that is worth memorizing:

> If you expect people to be in on the landing,
> include them for the takeoff.[9]

In addition to insights on assumptions—a neglected key component for stewarding your resources and preventing flops—you'll enjoy reading and repeating many of Rumsfeld's 400 rules, including:

- "The first consideration for meetings is whether to call one at all."

- "If you can find something everyone agrees on, it's wrong." (Rep. Mo Udall)

- "The default tendency in any bureaucracy, especially in government, is to substitute discussion for decision-making. The act of calling a meeting about a problem can in some cases be confused with actually doing something."

- "Stubborn opposition to proposals often has no basis other than the complaining question, 'Why wasn't I consulted?'" (Pat Moynihan)

- "If you don't know what your top three priorities are, you don't have priorities."

- "What you measure improves."[10]

We end with this caution about fake news! Peter Drucker, often called "the world's greatest management thinker," famously said, "What everyone knows is usually wrong." [11] William Cohen's book, *The Practical Drucker*, notes:

> What Drucker wanted to emphasize was that we must always question our assumptions, no matter from where they originate. This is especially so regarding anything that a majority of people "know" or assume without questioning. This "knowledge" should always be suspect and needs to be examined closer because, in a surprisingly high percentage of cases, the information "known to be true" will turn out to be inaccurate or completely false. This can lead to extremely poor, even disastrous management decisions. [12]

BOARDROOM LESSON

Identify your key assumptions
so your inaccurate premises don't lead to inaccurate
conclusions and colossal flops!
Invest time in assessing the validity of your assumptions—
and asking for advice and counsel from others.
Expect God to lead you to colleagues, acquaintances,
and even experts who will give you feedback
on your ministry's important plans
and your assumptions about those plans.

Board Action Steps:

○ 1. **Allocate:** Begin your process by allocating 30 minutes at your next board meeting to discuss assumptions. Ask board members and senior team members to read this lesson in advance—and then, in groups of two or three, ask each group to identify their key assumptions (up to 10).

○ 2. **Assess:** Ask the CEO and senior team to combine and narrow down the lists of assumptions—and give the board the first draft of the one-page document, "Our Top-10 Assumptions: The Radar Report."

○ 3. **Advise:** After the board affirms or edits the first draft, then it's time to review the Radar Report with others. Be intentional about seeking the advice and counsel of colleagues, friends, acquaintances, experts, givers, volunteers, former board and staff members, and others. The feedback will sharpen your plan.

Prayer
Lord, protect us from colossal flops!
Give us humility as we seek the counsel and
advice of others so that we follow Your plans.
Guide us to the correct premises that will lead us
to Kingdom impact for Your glory.
Amen.

40 | YOU MADE ME BETTER THAN I WAS

Board experiences should leave all participants better than they were.

Grant us the joy of arriving at adjournment close to one another because we are closer to You.[1]

Dan Bolin

In 1979, 20,000 of Muhammad Ali's "closest friends" assembled at the Great Western Forum in Inglewood, California, as a tribute to the great boxer and his career. Speaking of the loquacious Ali, Comedian Billy Crystal said, "There are few things that I can say about Ali that he has not already said about himself."

Crystal went on to perform "15 Rounds," a 12-minute routine tracing Ali's global, professional debut at the 1960 Olympics all the way up through his triumphant rematch against Leon Spinks in 1978, at the age of 36. Crystal switched flawlessly between impressions of sports commentator Howard Cosell, Ali, and others over the course of 15 vignettes—each made distinct by the ringing of a bell.

Ali always referred to Crystal as "Little Brother." After Crystal completed his routine that night, Ali gave him a hug and whispered in his ear, "Little brother, *you made my life better than it was.*"

In 2016, Crystal also spoke at Ali's funeral at the largest arena in Louisville, Kentucky and revealed for the first time what Ali had whispered to him in 1979. Crystal finished his touching eulogy by saying, "But didn't he make all of our lives a little bit better than they were?"

In the same way, shouldn't the time that board members and the CEO spend with each other make each of their lives a little better than they were? I think so.

How can boards and CEOs ensure that the boardroom experience will make everyone better than they were? It all starts with relationships.

I remember my shock (and that's not too strong a word) when two long-serving members of a small board were chatting before the meeting began. "Remind me again," one board member asked of the other board member, "what company do you work for?"

> *What distinguishes exemplary boards is that they are robust, effective social systems.*

After so much time serving together, these individuals should have known each other intimately, and as often happens on great boards, they could have become close friends. Yet it wasn't happening.

Jeffrey Sonnenfeld, in his article "What Makes Great Boards Great," says the key to board effectiveness "isn't structural, it's social." He adds, "The most involved, diligent, value-adding boards may or may not follow every recommendation in the good-governance handbook. What distinguishes exemplary boards is that they are robust, effective social systems."[2]

Max De Pree said, "Many people seem to feel that a good board structure enables high performance. This is simply not so."[3] He suggests that high impact boards "spend reflective time together, they are vulnerable with each other, they challenge each other in love, and deal with conflicts as mature adults."[4] The CEO and the board chair are "to set the tone for good relationships, but it is up to every individual on the board to develop, nurture, and polish good relationships."[5]

Here are just a few ways to make board members and CEOs better than they were before their boardroom involvement:

- **Unwavering support.** *Boards that are better* today than they were before know they can count on each other for support when the going gets tough.

- **Creative thought.** *Boards that are better* today than they were before are open to outside-the-box thinking. They have become about clock building, not time-telling.

- **Wrestling with issues that require wisdom.** *Boards that are better* than they were before recognize the difference between problems that require solutions and reports that invite feedback.

- **Robust interaction and guaranteed confidentiality.** *Boards that are better* than they were before give space for robust interaction and guaranteed confidentiality. If confidentiality is assured but then breached, the necessary interaction is muted.

BOARDROOM LESSON

The goal of every board should be to create an atmosphere where the board is better than it was before.

Board Action Steps:

○ 1. **Assess:** What is our board doing that makes us all better than we were before? Or is this not yet being accomplished?

○ 2. **Action Steps:** Identify action steps to maximize the board's social systems.

○ 3. **Anticipate:** Anticipate the high impact that will result from developing, nurturing, and polishing good relationships.

Prayer
Lord, may one of the key priorities of our board be
to set the tone for good relationships
and great board experiences.
Amen.

HOW HEALTHY IS YOUR BOARD?

Assessing your board's performance
is the first step to improving it.

> *The secret of effectiveness is to know what really counts,*
> *then do what really counts,*
> *and not worry about all the rest.*[1]
>
> Rick Warren

How would you rate your board's recent performance?
Evaluating the performance of boards is not as common as
it should be. Here's why:

- It takes too long and boards do not have time to spare.

- Ministries fail to recognize the importance of the
evaluation concept.

- There is a lack of easy-to-use evaluation tools.

- Ministries think, "We are doing pretty well right now."
(Remember: Good is the enemy of great!)

We hear you. So ECFA has developed an online tool called
NonprofitBoardScore™ to help your board evaluate its
performance. It is very easy to use, absolutely free, and only
takes a few minutes to complete.

NonprofitBoardScore™ gives you instant feedback, lets you take the evaluation over and over (you may want to take it every six months or annually), and allows you to save and print the results to share with your board, including a matrix reflecting the results specific to your ministry.

NonprofitBoardScore™ Sample Matrix

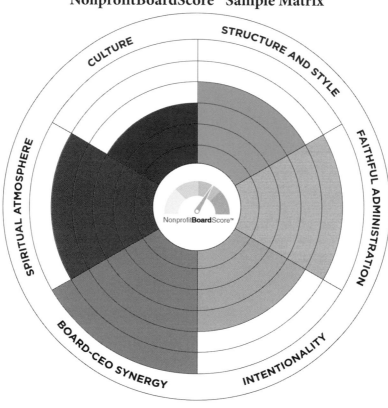

www.ECFA.org/Score

What does NonprifitBoardScore™ cover? We look at it this way. Board work is multi-faceted, and we have identified six interrelated elements. Understanding the relative health of

each element can help your board make progress across all
the elements:

Governance Elements	Sample Topics Included
1 Spiritual Atmosphere	Scripture reading, prayer, discernment, silence, Christ-centered character, spiritual gifts inventory, humble service, and loving community of grace and truth
2 Board-CEO Synergy	Regular fellowship, attention to physical health and soul care, board assessment, and annual review of CEO's performance and compensation/benefits
3 Intentionality	Clear agendas, Board Policies Manual, Prime Responsibility Chart, 80/20 focus on strategy, risk prioritization, and protection of all God's children from abuse
4 Faithful Administration	Avoid conflicts of interest, implement controls to prevent fraud and properly handle designated gifts, budget responsibly, and report with appropriate transparency
5 Structure and Style	Committed chair, board size, majority of independent board members, roles and responsibilities, meeting frequency, and annual commitment form
6 Culture	Spirit-led, mission-minded, self-disciplined, proactive, respectful, keen listeners, lifelong learners, integrity, accountability, confidentiality, and full of grace and truth

Every board governance element matters because each one
affects all the others. Your board culture will impact your

BOARDROOM LESSON

NonprofitBoardScore™ is an overall evaluation
of how your board is performing. It is not a substitute
for board members performing a self-assessment
of their own work or the more rare peer-to-peer evaluation,
where board members evaluate each other.

Board Action Steps:

○ 1. **Assess:** Have your CEO and every board member
take the survey at *ECFA.org/Score.* Save and print the
results to review at your next board meeting.

○ 2. **Analyze:** As you review areas of strength and
weakness, remember that even areas of strength can
be improved, but attending to the weaker areas first
will produce the most dramatic improvements.

○ 3. **Revisit:** Repeat the survey in six months or a year and
compare the results. Are the steps you've taken making
a difference?

Prayer
Lord, as we take inventory of our board's health,
please help us to know what really counts,
then to do what really counts.
Amen.

8 WAYS TO USE THIS BOOK IN YOUR MINISTRY

Here are eight ways to leverage the insights in this book and enrich the governance experience for your board:

1. **Give a copy to all newly elected board members.** This book can shape your board culture.

2. **Assign reading in the book.** Ask everyone to share three lessons they plan to read in the coming month.

3. **Appoint a "Leaders Are Readers Champion."** Discern which board member has the greatest passion for inspiring your board to be lifelong learners in effective Christ-centered governance. Ask that person to study this book thoroughly in order to keep governance topics and trends on your board's front burner. Ensure that every board member reads at least one governance book a year.[1]

4. **Highlight the Top-5 boardroom lessons.** Provide your board a "read-and-reflect" worksheet for the five topics that are most critical for the board to address in the next three to six months. At each board meeting, facilitate a discussion on at least one high-priority topic. (See the next idea.)

5. **Invest "10 minutes for governance" in every board meeting.** In every board meeting, remind board members that good governance does not happen by osmosis. It happens only with intentionality, training, and keeping critical governance topics (like focusing on policies, not

operations) on everyone's radar. After reading this book, select your Top-5 topics to address at future board meetings this year. Set a timer for 10 minutes and end promptly at the buzzer. This Governance 101 briefing will engage your board members—and remind them at each meeting that lifelong governance learning is important. Be sure to rotate the leadership so several board members have the privilege of being 10-minute facilitators.[2]

6. **Highlight boardroom lessons at your next retreat.** Prior to your next board retreat, give a copy of *More Lessons From the Nonprofit Boardroom* to each board member and invite every board member to read and review their favorite lesson. Limit each lesson review to 10 minutes: five minutes for the lesson highlights and five minutes for discussion. Sprinkle the reviews throughout the retreat and have a flipchart ready for listing next steps.

7. **Read *Lessons From the Nonprofit Boardroom* together.** When your board has read or highlighted the most relevant lessons in *More Lessons From the Nonprofit Boardroom*, then inspire your board members (especially new board members) to present several relevant reminders from the first book in this series (now in its second edition).

8. **Assess your board's performance with NonprofitBoardScore™.** This online tool is easy to use. The dashboard results may be the basis for starting important board discussions.

ENDNOTES

Introduction

[1] Tom Peters, *The Excellence Dividend: Meeting the Tech Tide with Work That Wows and Jobs That Last* (New York: Penguin Random House, 2018), xv–xvi.

[2] Michael Lee Stallard, Jason Pankau, and Katharine P. Stallard, *Connection Culture: The Competitive Advantage of Shared Identity, Empathy, and Understanding at Work* (Alexandria, VA: ATD Press, 2015), 44.

[3] Jeffrey A. Sonnenfeld, "What Makes Great Boards Great," Posted September 2002. *Harvard Business Review: https://hbr.org/2002/09/what-makes-great-boards-great.*

Part 1 – The Powerful Impact of Highly Engaged Boards

[1] Max De Pree, *Leadership Is an Art* (New York: Random House, 2014), 11.

Lesson 1 – Big Blessings Abound When Governance Faithfulness Flourishes

[1] Gary G. Hoag, R. Scott Rodin, and Wesley K. Willmer, *The Choice: The Christ-Centered Pursuit of Kingdom Outcomes* (Winchester, VA: ECFAPress, 2014), 31.

[2] John Pearson, "Big Blessings Abound When Management Faithfulness Flourishes," *Christian Management Report* (April 2004), 1.

[3] Warren Bird, *Unleashing Your Board's Potential: Comprehensive Report from ECFA's Nonprofit Governance Survey* (Winchester, VA: ECFAPress, 2019), 27. Visit *http://www.ECFA.org/Content/Surveys.*

Lesson 2 –Engage Board Members in Generative Thinking

[1] Attributed to Bill Ryan speaking at PricewaterhouseCoopers' Toronto office in October 2008, "Governance as Leadership: Key Concepts." Access Alliance: *https://accessalliance.ca/wp-content/uploads/2015/04/Strengthening-Leadership-and-Governance-for-NonProfit-Boards.pdf.*

[2] Richard P. Chait, William P. Ryan, and Barbara E. Taylor, *Governance as Leadership: Reframing the Work of Nonprofit Boards* (Hoboken, NJ: John Wiley & Sons, 2005).

[3] Ibid., 1–10.

[4] Ibid., 7.

[5] Ibid., 79.

[6] Ibid., 89.

[7] Ibid.

[8] Bird, *Unleash Your Board's Potential*, 9, 43. Just over half (59%) of ECFA boards agree that "Our board understands its governance role, but thoughtfully and regularly leverages the wisdom in the boardroom for 'generative thinking' (what some call the 'fuzzy front end' of product or program development)." Interestingly, according to internal ECFA data analysis, most growth occurs in organizations led by boards that excel at generative governance.

Lesson 3 – The Productivity Payoff of Intentional Hospitality

[1] Max De Pree, *Called to Serve: Creating and Nurturing the Effective Volunteer Board* (Grand Rapids, MI: William B. Eerdmans Publishing, 2001), 69.

[2] Ibid., 3.

[3] Bruce Bugbee, *What You Do Best in the Body of Christ: Discover Your Spiritual Gifts, Personal Style, and God-Given Passion*, rev. and exp. ed. (Grand Rapids, MI: Zondervan, 2005), 50.

[4] De Pree, *Called to Serve*, 26.

[5] Ibid., 11–12.

[6] Ibid., 18–19.

[7] Ibid., 85–87.

[8] Ibid., 22.

[9] De Pree, *Leadership Is an Art*, 11.

[10] Dan Busby and John Pearson, *Lessons From the Nonprofit Boardroom: 40 Insights for Better Board Meetings*, 2nd Ed. (Winchester, VA: ECFAPress, 2018), 202–206.

[11] John Pearson, "Called to Serve: No Board Detail Is Too Small (Index to 30 Blogs)," October 9, 2017, *http://ecfagovernance.blogspot.com/2017/10/called-to-serve-no-board-detail-is-too.html.*

Lesson 4 – Guarding Your CEO's Soul

[1] Ruth Haley Barton, *Strengthening the Soul of Your Leadership: Seeking God in the Crucible of Ministry*, exp. ed. (Downers Grove, IL: InterVarsity Press, 2018), 13.

[2] Jenni Hoag, "Soul Care." Soulcare Anchoress: *http://soulcareanchoress.com/soul-care-definitions/.*

[3] Bird, *Unleash Your Board's Potential*, 14, 22, 31, 36-37, 53.

[4] Stephen A. Macchia's informal communications with the authors.

[5] Dan Busby, TRUST: *The Firm Foundation for Kingdom Fruitfulness* (Winchester, VA: ECFAPress, 2015), 8.

[6] Andrew Murray, *Humility: The Beauty of Holiness* (Radford, VA: Wilder, 2008), 9.

[7] Ralph Enlow, *The Leader's Palette: Seven Primary Colors* (Bloomington, IN: WestBow, 2013), 118.

[8] Dallas Willard with Don Simpson, *Revolution of Character: Discovering Christ's Pattern for Spiritual Transformation* (Colorado Springs: NavPress, 2005), 51.

[9] Stephen A. Macchia, "Recent Revelations Lead Us Back to Trusted Pathways," *Leadership Transformations* (blog), August 10, 2018, *http://www.leadershiptransformations.org/blog/?p=1552.*

[10] John Ortberg, *Soul Keeping: Caring for the Most Important Part of You* (Grand Rapids, MI: Zondervan, 2014), 140.

[11] R. Glenn Ball and Darrell Puls, *Let Us Prey: The Plague of Narcissist Pastors and What We Can Do About It* (Eugene, OR: Cascade, 2017).

[12] Stephen A. Macchia, *Broken and Whole: A Leader's Path to Spiritual Transformation* (Downers Grove, IL: InterVarsity Press, 2016).

Part 2 – Boardroom Tools and Templates

[1] Quoted in *Scaling Up: How a Few Companies Make It...and Why the Rest Don't – Mastering the Rockefeller Habits 2.0* by Verne Harnish (Gazelles, 2014), 1.

Lesson 5 – Dashboards Are Not a Secret Sauce to Sound Governance

[1] Ralph Waldo Emerson, *The Complete Works of Ralph Waldo Emerson: Lectures and Biographical Sketches* (San Bernardino, CA: Ulan Press, 2012), 21.

[2] Harnish, *Scaling Up*, 170–71.

[3] Max De Pree, *Leading Without Power: Finding Hope in Serving Community* (San Francisco: Jossey-Bass, 1997), 47.

[4] Dan Busby and John Pearson, *ECFA Tools and Templates for Effective Board Governance: Time Saving Solutions for Your Board* (Winchester, VA: ECFAPress, 2019), 103–10.

Lesson 6 – Enhance Harmony by Clarifying Your Participant-Hat Expectations

[1] *ECFA Governance Toolbox Series No. 2: Balancing Board Roles— Understanding the 3 Board Hats: Governance, Volunteer, Participant* (Winchester, VA: ECFAPress, 2013). Visit: *www.ECFA.org/Toolbox.*

[2] Visit the ECFA Knowledge Center, *ECFA.org/KnowledgeCenter* for a sample board member annual affirmation statement. *http://www.ECFA.org/Content/Board-Member-Annual-Affirmation-Statement-NP.*

[3] Used by permission of the author, Al Newell, at *www.newellandassociates.com.*

[4] Busby and Pearson, *ECFA Tools and Templates for Effective Board Governance,* 225–36.

Lesson 7 – Eliminate Fuzziness Between Board and Staff Roles

[1] Ram Charan, *Owning Up: The 14 Questions Every Board Member Needs to Ask* (San Francisco: Jossey-Bass, 2009), 164.

[2] Bird, *Unleash Your Board's Potential,* 21.

[3] Busby and Pearson, *Lessons From the Nonprofit Boardroom,* 16–22. See also Busby and Pearson, *ECFA Tools and Templates for Effective Board Governance,* 171-74. This book provides access to the Board Policies Manual template.

[4] The "Prime Responsibility Chart" is adapted from Chapter 18, "The Operations Buckets," by John Pearson, *Mastering the Management Buckets* (Ventura, CA: Regal, 2008), 232. An executive at The Boeing Company, who was also a board member at SAMBICA in Bellevue, WA, adapted the Boeing template for use by the camp's board.

[5] Charan, *Owning Up*, 165.

[6] Access the Prime Responsibility Chart (PRC) by purchasing *ECFA Tools and Templates for Effective Board Governance* by Busby and Pearson.

Lesson 8 – Design Your Succession Plan—NOW!

[1] From the foreword by John C. Maxwell in Tom Mullins, *Passing the Leadership Baton: A Winning Transition Plan for Your Ministry* (Nashville, TN: Thomas Nelson/Leadership Network, 2015), xiv.

[2] William Vanderbloemen and Warren Bird, *NEXT: Pastoral Succession That Works* (Grand Rapids, MI: Baker, 2014), 9.

[3] Bird, *Unleash Your Board's Potential*, 24, 25, 28, 31, 44.

[4] David McKenna, *Stewards of a Sacred Trust: CEO Selection, Transition and Development for Boards of Christ-centered Organizations* (Winchester, VA: ECFAPress, 2010), 19.

[5] *ECFA Governance Toolbox Series No. 4: Succession Planning—Eleven Principles for Successful Successions* (Winchester, VA: ECFAPress, 2017). Visit: *www.ECFA.org/Toolbox*.

[6] Peter F. Drucker with Joseph A. Maciariello, *The Daily Drucker: 366 Days of Insight and Motivation for Getting the Right Things Done* (New York: HarperBusiness, 2004), 112.

[7] R. Scott Rodin, *The Steward Leader: Transforming People, Organizations and Communities* (Downers Grove, IL: InterVarsity Press, 2010), 13–14.

[8] Vanderbloemen and Bird, *NEXT*, 33.

[9] Nancy Axelrod, *Chief Executive Succession Planning: Essential Guidance for Boards and CEOs*, 2nd ed. (Washington, DC: BoardSource, 2010), 2.

[10] Bill Conaty and Ram Charan, *The Talent Masters: Why Smart Leaders Put People Before Numbers* (New York: Crown Publishing, 2010), 2.

[11] Barton, *Strengthening the Soul of Your Leadership*, 198.

[12] Donald Rumsfeld, *Rumsfeld's Rules: Leadership Lessons in Business, Politics, War, and Life* (New York: HarperCollins Publishers, 2013), 59.

[13] Quoting Michael J. Lotito in Janet Boydell, Barry Deutsch, and Brad Remillard, *You're Not the Person I Hired! A CEO's Survival Guide to Hiring Top Talent* (Bloomington, IN: AuthorHouse, 2006), 41.

[14] Ram Charan, *Owning Up*, 68.

[15] "Facilitator Guide" in *ECFA Governance Toolbox Series No. 4: Succession Planning—Eleven Principles for Successful Successions* (Winchester, VA: ECFAPress, 2017), 3. Visit: *www.ECFA.org/Toolbox*.

Part 3 – Nominees for the Board Member Hall of Fame

[1] Patrick Lencioni is quoted in Jim Brown, *The Imperfect Board Member: Discovering the Seven Disciplines of Governance Excellence* (San Francisco: Jossey-Bass, 2006), xi.

Lesson 9 – Just Do One Thing a Month

[1] *ECFA Governance Toolbox Series No. 2: Balancing Board Roles.*

Lesson 11 – Thrive With Four Kingdom Values

[1] Frederick Buechner is quoted in Stephen A. Macchia, *Crafting a Rule of Life: An Invitation to a Well-Ordered Way* (Downers Grove, IL: InterVarsity Press, 2012), 54.

[2] John Pellowe, *Serving as a Board Member: Practical Guidance for Directors of Christian Ministries* (Elmira, ON, Canada: Canadian Council of Christian Charities, 2012), 4–5.

[3] Ibid., 4.

[4] Macchia, *Crafting a Rule of Life*, 62.

[5] David L. McKenna, *Call of the Chair: Leading the Board of the Christ-centered Ministry* (Winchester, VA: ECFAPress, 2017), 71.

[6] Ibid.

[7] Bugbee, *What You Do Best in the Body of Christ*.

[8] Visit *https://www.gallupstrengthscenter.com* for the *Discover Your CliftonStrengths* assessment, previously available as *StrengthsFinder 2.0* in book form and online. A faith-based resource, recommended by John C. Maxwell, is also available: Albert L. Winseman, Donald O. Clifton, and Curt Liesveld, *Living Your Strengths: Discover Your God-Given Talents and Inspire Your Community*, exp. ed. (New York, NY: Gallup Press, 2008).

[9] For more on the four social styles, visit *http://tracom.com/social-style-training/model* or read the faith-based resource, *How to Deal With Annoying People: What to Do When You Can't Avoid Them* by Bob Phillips and Kimberly Alyn (Eugene, OR: Harvest House, 2005).

[10] Frederick Buechner is quoted in Macchia, *Crafting a Rule of Life*, 54.

[11] *Chariots of Fire* directed by Hugh Hudson (1981: United Kingdom: Warner Home Video, 2005), DVD.

[12] For more resources, access and download "Tent Cards and Tools for Leveraging Board Member Strengths" in Busby and Pearson, *ECFA Tools and Templates for Effective Board Governance*, 217-23.

[13] *Chariots of Fire* directed by Hugh Hudson.

Lesson 12 – Keeping the Boardroom Afloat

[1] Robert C. Andringa and Ted W. Engstrom, *Nonprofit Board Answer Book: Practical Guidelines for Board Members and Chief Executives* (Washington, DC: National Center for Nonprofit Boards, 1997), 158. (Note: NCNB is now known as BoardSource.)

[2] ECFA unpublished 2019 research.

Part 4 – Epiphanies in the Boardroom

[1] Michael Hyatt, *Your Best Year Ever: A 5-Step Plan for Achieving Your Most Important Goals* (Grand Rapids, MI: Baker, 2018), 160.

Lesson 13 – Caution! Understand the Governance Pendulum Principle

[1] John Pellowe, *Serving as a Board Members*, 19.

[2] Chait, Ryan, and Taylor, *Governance as Leadership*, 58.

[3] Bird, *Unleash Your Board's Potential*, 33.

[4] Quoted in Bob Kelly, *Protected! A True Life Story of God's Word Smuggled Behind the Iron Curtain—and the Influence of a "Tremendous" Man* (Boiling Springs, PA: Tremendous Leadership, 2018), 104.

[5] Rodin, *The Steward Leader*, 2010.

Lesson 14 – Plant a Seed in the Boardroom

[1] Richard Kriegbaum, *Leadership Prayers* (Wheaton, IL: Tyndale House, 1998), 38.

Lesson 15 – Be Intentional About Your First 30 Minutes

[1] Chip Heath and Dan Heath, *The Power of Moments: Why Certain Experiences Have Extraordinary Impact* (New York: Simon & Schuster, 2017), 89.

[2] Ibid., 265.

[3] Don Cousins, Leith Anderson, and Arthur DeKruyter, *Mastering Church Management* (Portland, OR: Multnomah Press, 1990), 17.

[4] Heath and Heath, *The Power of Moments*.

Lesson 16 – Looking for Consensus but Finding Division

[1] Andringa and Engstrom, *Nonprofit Board Answer Book*, 150.

[2] "Consensus." Merriam-Webster: *https://www.merriam-webster.com/dictionary/consensus*.

[3] Busby and Pearson, *ECFA Tools and Templates for Effective Board Governance*, 243-46.

[4] Andringa and Engstrom, *Nonprofit Board Answer Book*, 151.

[5] Ibid.

[6] ECFA unpublished 2019 research.

[7] McKenna, *Call of the Chair*.

Part 5 – Boardroom Bloopers

[1] Bob Buford, *Drucker & Me: What a Texas Entrepreneur Learned from the Father of Modern Management* (Brentwood, TN: Worthy, 2014), 137.

Lesson 17 – Botched Executive Sessions Are Not Pretty

[1] John Carver and Miriam Mayhew Carver, *Basic Principles of Policy Governance: Carver Guide 1* (San Francisco: Jossey-Bass, 1996), 2.

[2] Ibid.

Lesson 18 – Warning! Resumé-Builders Make Lousy Board Members

[1] De Pree, *Called to Serve*, 19-20.

[2] Ibid. For an index to 30 short blogs by John Pearson, based on Max De Pree's book, *Called to Serve*, visit *http://ecfagovernance.blogspot.com/2017/10/called-to-serve-no-board-detail-is-too.html*.

[3] *ECFA Governance Toolbox Series No. 1: Recruiting Board Members—Leveraging the 4 Phases of Board Recruitment: Cultivation, Recruitment, Orientation, Engagement* (Winchester, VA: ECFAPress, 2012).

Lesson 19 – Beware the Phone-Book-Size Report

[1] Ram Charan, Dennis Carey and Michael Useem, *Boards That Lead: When to Take Charge, When to Partner, and When to Stay Out of the Way*, (Boston: Harvard Business Review Press, 2014), 93.

[2] Sonnenfeld, "What Makes Great Boards Great."

[3] Ibid.

[4] Ibid., 7.

[5] Ibid., 6.

Part 6 – Boardroom Time-Wasters, Troublemakers, and Truth-Tellers

[1] Dr. Henry Cloud, *Necessary Endings: The Employees, Businesses, and Relationships That All of Us Have to Give Up in Order to Move Forward* (New York: HarperCollins, 2010), 24.

Lesson 20 – Don't Be Late—or Annoying!

[1] Ruth Haley Barton, *Pursuing God's Will Together: A Discernment Practice for Leadership Groups* (Downers Grove, IL: InterVarsity Press, 2012), 207.

[2] Busby and Pearson, *ECFA Tools and Templates for Effective Board Governance*, 243-46.

Lesson 21 – Alert! The ER Factor Causes Value Extraction

[1] Randy Ross and David Salyers, *Remarkable!: Maximizing Results through Value Creation* (Grand Rapids, MI: Baker, 2016), 104.

[2] Ibid., 117.

[3] Ibid.

Lesson 22 – Whopper Mistakes Can Unravel Your Ministry

[1] Max De Pree, *Leadership Is an Art*, 11.

[2] Michael Watkins, *The First 90 Days: Critical Success Strategies for New Leaders at All Levels* (Boston: Harvard Business School Press, 2003), 61. Note: Board members must discern not only what CEO competencies they need in a CEO for the future, but what kind of situation their new leader will inherit—and whether the candidate has relevant experience. The author's "STARS" model describes four broad types of organizational situations: Start-up, Turn-Around, Realignment, and Sustaining Success.

Lesson 23 – The Bully in the Boardroom

[1] Bill Haslam, "Public Office as a Spiritual Discipline." Posted January 11, 2018. Comment: *https://www.cardus.ca/comment/article/5171/public-office-as-a-spiritual-discipline/*.

[2] See Thom Rainer, "Nine Traits of Church Bullies." Posted March 30, 2015. *https://thomrainer.com/2015/03/nine-traits-church-bullies/*. "Eight Warning Signs of a Bully Church Member." Posted July 20, 2016. *https://thomrainer.com/2016/07/eight-warning-signs-bully-church-member/*.

[3] Joe McKeever, "What to Say to a Church Bully." Posted September 24, 2013. Ministry Today: *www.ministrytodaymag.com*.

[4] Michael J. Anthony, *The Effective Church Board* (Eugene, OR: Wipf and Stock Publishers, 2000), 266.

[5] The term "bully pulpit" was coined by United States President Theodore Roosevelt, who referred to his office as a "bully pulpit," by which he meant a terrific platform from which to advocate an agenda. See "Bully Pulpit." Merriam-Webster: *https://www.merriam-webster.com/dictionary/bully pulpit*.

[6] Ruth Haley Barton addresses a Matthew 18 spiritual discernment process, "Practicing Conflict Transformation," in her book *Pursuing God's Will Together*, 145–148.

[7] Thom Rainer, "Nine Ways to Deal With Church Bullies." Posted April 1, 2015. *https://thomrainer.com/2015/04/nine-ways-deal-church-bullies/*.

[8] Kerry Patterson, et. al., *Crucial Conversations: Tools for Talking When Stakes Are High*, 2nd ed. (Columbus, OH: McGraw-Hill Education, 2011).

Part 7 – Boardroom Best Practices

[1] Quoted in Ruth Haley Barton, *Invitation to Retreat: The Gift and Necessity of Time Away with God* (Downers Grove, IL: InterVarsity Press, 2018), 111.

Lesson 24 – Should Most Standing Committees Stand Down?

[1] Richard P. Chait, Thomas P. Holland, and Barbara E. Taylor, *Improving the Performance of Governing Boards* (Westport, CT: American Council on Education/Oryx Press, 1996), 1–2.

Lesson 26 – Big Rocks, Pebbles, and Sand

[1] Aubrey Malphurs, *Leading Leaders: Empowering Church Boards of Ministry Excellence* (Grand Rapids, MI: Baker, 2005), 69.

[2] Stephen R. Covey, *First Things First* (New York: Simon & Schuster, 1996), 88–89.

[3] Ibid.

[4] Ibid., 110.

[5] Bird, *Unleash Your Board's Potential*, 35, 39.

Lesson 27 – Address Absentee Board Member Syndrome

[1] Cousins, Anderson, and DeKruyter, *Mastering Church Management*, 17.

[2] *ECFA Governance Toolbox Series No. 1.* "The Board Member Annual Affirmation Statement" can also be downloaded by purchasing the book by Busby and Pearson, *ECFA Tools and Templates for Effective Board Governance.*

[3] Busby and Pearson, *ECFA Tools and Templates for Effective Board Governance*, 231-42.

[4] Busby and Pearson, *Lessons From the Nonprofit Boardroom*, 16–22.

[5] Used by permission of the author, Al Newell, at *www.newellandassociates.com.*

[6] Adapted from John Pearson, "7 Ways to Address Absentee Board Member Syndrome." *Governance of Christ-Centered Organizations* (blog), October 25, 2017. *http://ecfagovernance. blogspot.com/2017/10/7-ways-to-address-absentee-board-member.html.*

Part 8 – Boardroom Worst Practices

[1] Mckenna, *Call of the Chair*, 17.

Lesson 28 – Defending Risks Everywhere Is Not a Strategic Plan

[1] Adapted from Sun Tzu, *The Art of War* (Value Classic Reprints, 2016), 17. This quote is based on the more literal translation of Sun Tzu's caution: "If he sends reinforcements everywhere, he will everywhere be weak."

[2] Rosemarie Jarski, *Words from the Wise: Over 1,000 of the Smartest Things Ever Said* (New York: Skyhorse, 2007), 430.

[3] Bird, *Unleash Your Board's Potential*, 21.

[4] Pearson, *Mastering the Management Buckets*, 182.

[5] Gary Keller with Jay Papasan, *The ONE Thing: The Surprisingly Simple Truth Behind Extraordinary Results* (Austin, TX: Bard, 2012), 1–3.

Lesson 30 – Are You Competing Based on Overhead— Really?

[1] Busby, *TRUST*, 105.

[2] "Let's Admit It—The Emperor Is Naked: Functional Expense Reporting for Nonprofit Organizations Is Voodoo." Posted January 6, 2013. Batts Morrison Wales & Lee: *https://www.nonprofitcpa.com/lets-admit-it-the-emperor-is-naked-functional-expense-reporting-for-nonprofit-organizations-is-voodoo/.*

[3] Ibid.

Lesson 31 – Where Two or Three Are Gathered on Social Media . . .

[1] *ECFA Governance Toolbox Series No. 3: Conflicts of Interest—Addressing Board and Organizational Conflicts of Interest: Avoiding Trouble, Trouble,*

Trouble with Related-Party Transactions (Winchester, VA: ECFAPress, 2015). Visit: *www.ECFA.org/Toolbox.*

Part 9 – Holy Ground and Other Locations

[1] John Baillie, *A Diary of Private Prayer* (New York: Scribner, 1949), 21.

Lesson 32 – There Are Two Things You Should Never Joke About – #1: Prayer

[1] Barton, *Strengthening the Soul of Your Leadership*, 124.

[2] John Pearson, "The Meeting Before the Meeting," *Governance of Christ-Centered Organizations* (blog), March 8, 2013, *http://ecfagovernance.blogspot.com/2013/03/the-meeting-before-meeting.html.*

[3] Olan Hendrix, "Two Things Boards Should Never Joke About." Reprinted with permission from *CMA Management Monthly*, published by Christian Management Association, now Christian Leadership Alliance (May 1999).

[4] Ibid.

[5] C. H. Spurgeon, *Spurgeon's Sermons on Prayer* (Peabody, MA: Hendrickson, 2007), 96.

Lesson 33 – There Are Two Things You Should Never Joke About – #2: Fundraising

[1] R. Scott Rodin, *The Third Conversion: A Novelette* (Colbert, WA: Kingdom Life, 2011), 89–90.

[2] Hendrix, "Two Things Boards Should Never Joke About."

[3] Rodin, *The Third Conversion*, 86.

[4] Ibid., 97–98.

[5] R. Scott Rodin and Gary G. Hoag, *The Sower: Redefining the Ministry of Raising Kingdom Resources* (Winchester, VA: ECFAPress, 2016).

[6] Bird, *Unleashing Your Board's Potential*. Visit *http://www.ECFA.org/Content/Surveys.*

Lesson 34 – Five Troublesome Misconceptions of Board Members

[1] Bird, *Unleash Your Board's Potential*, 46.

[2] Anthony, *The Effective Church Board*, 35–40.

[3] Ibid., 36 (quoting Larry Osborne).

[4] Steve Stroope and Kurt Bruner, *Tribal Church: Lead Small, Impact BIG* (Nashville: B&H, 2012), 108.

[5] Thom S. Ranier and Eric Geiger, *Simple Church* (Nashville, TN: B&H, 2011), 200–1.

Lesson 35 – Leverage the 80/20 Rule in the Boardroom

[1] Drucker with Maciariello, *The Daily Drucker*, 269.

[2] Henry T. Blackaby and Claude V. King, *Experiencing God: Knowing and Doing the Will of God* (Nashville: LifeWay Press, 1990), 8.

[3] Busby and Pearson, *Lessons From the Nonprofit Boardroom*, 202-6. (See Lesson 39: "Invest '10 Minutes for Governance' in Every Board Meeting.")

[4] Peter F. Drucker, Frances Hesselbein, and Joan Snyder Kuhl, *Peter Drucker's Five Most Important Questions: Enduring Wisdom for Today's Leaders* (Hoboken, NJ: John Wiley & Sons, 2015), 35–45.

[5] See "Five-Finger Feedback" featured in Busby and Pearson, *ECFA Tools and Templates for Effective Board Governance*, 23–24.

[6] Richard Koch, *The 80/20 Principle: The Secret to Achieving More with Less* (New York: Doubleday, 2008).

[7] Bird, *Unleash Your Board's Potential*, 18, 30, 43.

[8] George S. Babbes and Michael Zigarelli, *The Minister's MBA: Essential Business Tools for Maximum Ministry Success* (Nashville: B&H, 2006), 119. (See pages 119–131, "The Strategy Map: Creating a Blueprint for Success.")

[9] Ibid., 127.

[10] Jim Collins, *Turning the Flywheel: Why Some Companies Build Momentum . . . and Others Don't* (New York: HarperCollins, 2019).

[11] See "The Rolling 3-Year Strategic Plan" featured in Busby and Pearson, *ECFA Tools and Templates for Effective Board Governance*, 149–66.

[12] See "Board Retreat Trend-Spotting Exercise" featured in Busby and Pearson, *ECFA Tools and Templates for Effective Board Governance*, 167–70.

[13] Charan, *Owning Up*, 57–71. (See Question 5 on owning the strategy.)

[14] Busby and Pearson, *Lessons From the Nonprofit Boardroom*, 198. See Lesson 38: "Great Boards Delegate Their Reading."

[15] Visit "The Strategy Bucket" webpage (*http://managementbuckets.com/ strategy-bucket*) for a short list of future-focused books recommended by John Pearson, including *The Attacker's Advantage: Turning Uncertainty into Breakthrough Opportunities* by Ram Charan.

[16] Barton, *Pursuing God's Will Together*, 99.

[17] Gordon Flinn, "Week 42: Halftime Is An Entrepreneurial Enterprise," *Drucker Mondays* (blog), Oct. 20, 2015, *https://urgentink.typepad.com/ drucker_mondays/2015/10/week-42-halftime-is-an-entrepreneurial- enterprise.html*. Flinn's blog was one of 52 color commentaries by 52 ministry leaders on the book, Joseph A. Maciariello, *A Year With Peter Drucker: 52 Weeks of Coaching for Leadership Effectiveness* (New York: HarperBusiness, 2014), 330.

Part 10 – Building a 24/7 Board Culture

[1] John Pellowe, *Serving as a Board Member*, 37.

Lesson 36 – Watch Out for Boards Asleep at the Wheel

[1] See *10 Essentials of Giver-Restricted Gifts to Ministries*, ECFA: *www.ECFA.org/EBooks.aspx*.

[2] See *9 Essentials of Ministry Cash Reserves*, ECFA: *www.ECFA.org/EBooks.aspx*.

[3] See *7 Essentials of Related-Party Transactions for Ministries*, ECFA: *www.ECFA.org/EBooks.aspx*.

Lesson 38 – Seven Times When a Board Member Should Bid Adieu

[1] Dr. Henry Cloud, *Necessary Endings: The Employees, Businesses, and Relationships That All of Us Have to Give Up in Order to Move Forward* (New York: HarperBusiness, 2010), 26.

Lesson 39 – Identify Your Key Assumptions

[1] Rumsfeld, *Rumsfeld's Rules*, 39.

[2] Ibid., 68–88.

[3] Ibid., 76.

[4] Ibid., 77–78.

[5] Ibid., 78.

[6] Read Steve Macchia's convicting insights in Lesson 11, "Tap! Tap! Tap!" in Busby and Pearson, *Lessons From the Nonprofit Boardroom*.

[7] R. Mark Dillon, *Giving & Getting in the Kingdom. A Field Guide* (Chicago: Moody Publishers, 2012), 65.

[8] Ibid.

[9] Rumsfeld, *Rumsfeld's Rules*, 299–331. (Note: Appendix B includes the master list of 400 Rumsfeld's Rules. The book includes color commentaries on dozens of Rumsfeld's favorite rules.)

[10] Ibid.

[11] William A. Cohen, *The Practical Drucker: Applying the Wisdom of the World's Greatest Management Thinker* (New York: AMACOM, 2014), 55–56. (Read Chapter 9, "What Everyone Knows Is Usually Wrong.")

[12] Ibid.

Lesson 40 – You Made Me Better Than I Was

[1] From "A Board Prayer" by Dan Bolin, featured in Lesson 40, *Lessons From the Nonprofit Boardroom*, 207–211.

[2] Sonnenfeld, "What Makes Great Boards Great," 4.

[3] Max De Pree, *Called to Serve*, 11.

[4] Ibid., 55.

[5] Ibid., 11.

Bonus Resource: How Healthy Is Your Board?

[1] Rick Warren, *The Purpose Driven Church: Every Church Is Big in God's Eyes* (Grand Rapids, MI: Zondervan, 1995), 87.

Study Guide: 8 Ways to Use This Book in Your Ministry

[1] Busby and Pearson, *Lessons From the Nonprofit Boardroom*, 198–201.

[2] Ibid., 202–6.

INDEX

ABOUT THE AUTHORS

DAN BUSBY

 Dan Busby is the President of ECFA (Evangelical Council for Financial Accountability) in Winchester, Virginia. He has been in leadership positions with ECFA for 20 years. Prior to coming to ECFA, Dan was the founding and managing partner of a CPA firm in the Kansas City area, and served in leadership positions with the University of Kansas Medical Center and The Wesleyan Church—International Headquarters. He has served over 110 man-years on nonprofit boards.

Dan is the author or co-author of 66 editions of 11 different titles plus numerous eBooks and booklets. Two titles published annually since 1991, the *Minister's Tax & Financial Guide* and the *Church and Nonprofit Tax & Financial Guide*, have set a standard as easy-to-understand resources on these topics. For the 2020 edition of these books, Michael Martin has joined him as a co-author.

In 2017, Dan teamed up with John Pearson to pen *Lessons From the Nonprofit Boardroom, Lessons From the Church Boardroom*, and *ECFA Tools and Templates for Effective Board Governance*. His book, *TRUST: The Firm Foundation for Kingdom Fruitfulness*, is a treasure trove linked to trust, based on Busby's wit and wisdom. *The Guide to Charitable Giving for Churches and Ministries*, co-authored by Busby, answers the important questions about the proper handling of charitable contributions for legal, tax, and accounting purposes.

An avid baseball fan and former umpire, the National Baseball Hall of Fame often consults with Dan concerning memorabilia acquisitions. His book about the New York Yankees, *Before and After Babe Ruth,* was published in 2018. His book about the Brooklyn Dodgers, *Before and After Jackie Robinson,* is scheduled for release in 2020.

Dan and his wife, Claudette, have two children, Julie and Alan, and three grandchildren. His top five strengths in the CliftonStrengths assessment are: Learner, Achiever, Connectedness, Ideation, and Belief. A survivor of living in "tornado alley" in Kansas until 1987, Dan has not sought shelter from tornadoes since leaving Kansas.

JOHN PEARSON

John Pearson is a board governance and management consultant from San Clemente, California. He served more than 30 years as a nonprofit ministry CEO, 25 of those years as the CEO of three national or international associations, including Christian Camp and Conference Association, Willow Creek Association (now Global Leadership Network), and Christian Management Association (now Christian Leadership Alliance).

He is the author of *Mastering the Management Buckets: 20 Critical Competencies for Leading Your Business or Nonprofit,* and the co-author with Dan Busby of *Lessons From the Nonprofit Boardroom*, *Lessons From the Church Boardroom*, and *ECFA Tools and Templates for Effective Board Governance*. He is also co-author with Dr. Robert Hisrich of *Marketing Your Ministry: 10 Critical Principles*.

John also writes an eNewsletter, *Your Weekly Staff Meeting*, and since 2006, he has reviewed more than 400 leadership and management books in his eNews. He writes a board blog for ECFA, "Governance of Christ-Centered Organizations," and is the creator of the *ECFA Governance Toolbox Series*. John also served five years as the lead facilitator of the M.J. Murdock Charitable Trust's Board Leadership & Development Program. He currently serves on the board of Christian Community Credit Union.

John and his wife, Joanne, have traveled and/or facilitated leadership, management and board governance training in more than 50 countries and are blessed to live close to their son Jason and daughter-in-law Melinda, and their five grandchildren (including triplet teenagers). His top five strengths in the CliftonStrengths assessment are: Focus, Responsibility, Significance, Belief, and Maximizer. A survivor of 21 winters in Chicago, John has not shoveled snow since 1994.

Visit John's website at *www.ManagementBuckets.com*.

ABOUT ECFA

Enhancing Trust

ECFA enhances trust in Christ-centered churches and ministries by establishing and applying Seven Standards of Responsible Stewardship™ to certified organizations.

Founded in 1979, ECFA provides accreditation to leading Christ-centered churches and other nonprofit organizations that faithfully demonstrate compliance with established standards for financial accountability, transparency, stewardship, and board governance. The Christ-centered ministries accredited by ECFA include churches, denominations, educational institutions, rescue missions, camps, and many other types of tax-exempt 501(c)(3) organizations. Collectively, these nearly 2,400 organizations represent over $29 billion in annual revenue.

ECFA accreditation entitles a ministry to use the ECFA seal and receive other benefits. The continuing use of the seal depends on the ministry's good faith compliance with all ECFA Standards.

Inspire your board members to follow the blog!
https://MoreLessonsNonprofitBoardroom.blogspot.com/

More Lessons From the Nonprofit Boardroom
Effectiveness. Excellence. Elephants!

40 Wednesdays. 40 Blogs. 40 Guest Bloggers!

SHORT COLOR COMMENTARIES ON THESE
ELEPHANTS IN THE BOARDROOM!

- ✓ Engage board members in generative thinking.
- ✓ Guarding your CEO's soul.
- ✓ Eliminate fuzziness between board and staff roles.
- ✓ Design your succession plan now!
- ✓ Caution! Understand the governance pendulum principle.

- ✓ Be intentional about your first 30 minutes.
- ✓ Botched executive sessions are not pretty.
- ✓ The bully in the boardroom!
- ✓ Where two or three are gathered on social media…
- ✓ Two things you should never joke about!

- ✓ Leverage The 80/20 Rule in the boardroom.
- ✓ Identify your key assumptions.

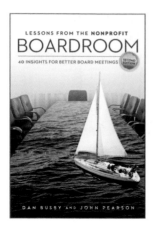

Lessons From the Nonprofit Boardroom: 40 Insights for Better Board Meetings, Second Edition by Dan Busby and John Pearson

This book is based on the wisdom and experience of two seasoned veterans in the Christ-centered nonprofit arena. Written in an engaging, easy-to read and understandable style, the authors provide 40 short lessons for inspiring your board in God-honoring governance.

- The Powerful Impact of Highly Engaged Boards
- Boardroom Tools, Templates, and Typos
- Nominees for the Boardroom Hall of Fame
- Epiphanies in the Boardroom
- Boardroom Bloopers
- Boardroom Time-Wasters, Troublemakers, and Truth-Tellers
- Boardroom Best Practices
- Holy Ground and Other Locations
- Building a 24/7 Board Culture
- Boards That Lead and Boards That Read

Discover how the role of preparation, policies, and most importantly, the Holy Spirit all converge in the boardroom.

"A Board Prayer"
Learn why many boards are reading
Lesson 40 at every board meeting.

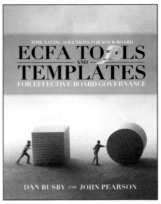

ECFA Tools and Templates for Effective Board Governance
by Dan Busby and John Pearson

If you knew that by leveraging a specific tool or a template it would exponentially enhance your communication, your outcomes, your results, and your governance joy— you'd do it, right? These "add-water-and-stir" practical tools will enhance your board's productivity.

All of the 22 tools in this 266-page book have been field tested in hundreds of boardrooms. Here is just a sampling of the downloadable templates including:

- Board Retreat Trend-Spotting Exercise
- Rolling 3-Year Strategic Plan Placemat
- Board Member Annual Affirmation Statement
- The Board's Annual Financial Management Audit
- The 5/15 Monthly Report to the Board
- Board Policies Manual

When you use these time-saving solutions, you'll wonder why you didn't discover them sooner.

Peter Drucker on Tool Competence:

Although I don't know a single for-profit business
that is as well managed as a few of the nonprofits,
the great majority of the nonprofits can be graded a 'C' at best.
Not for lack of effort; most of them work very hard.
But for lack of focus, and for lack of tool competence."

Available at ECFAPress • ECFA.org/ECFAPress

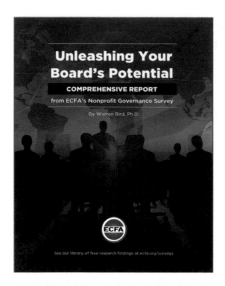

Unleashing Your Board's Potential: Comprehensive Report from ECFA's Nonprofit Governance Survey
by Warren Bird

What would you want to ask if you could sit down with 1,662 CEOs, board chairs, and board members from Christ-centered nonprofits – all ECFA-accredited ministries? We did just that with a huge survey and have compiled everyone's responses in *Unleashing Your Board's Potential: Comprehensive Report from ECFA's Nonprofit Governance Survey* by Warren Bird, Ph.D.

More than 50 illustrated pages highlight the key findings, all with a highly practical bent designed to help your ministry's board and leadership go to new levels of excellence and effectiveness. Topics include:

- What effective boards do best (spoiler: the first one relates to clarity of roles)

- Four top challenges to governance (spoiler: "succession planning" is one)

- Where CEO and board members aren't on the same page

- How many boards have a policy and process for removing an ineffective board member

The survey is available as a free download.

Available at ECFA.org/Surveys

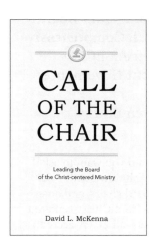

Call of the Chair: Leading the Board of the Christ-centered Ministry
by David L. McKenna

As Christ-centered ministries go through changing times, the leadership role of the board chair rises in significance. As manager of the board, the chair joins the CEO in responsibility for advancing the mission, partnering with the vision, governing by policy, and setting the tone for the morale of the ministry. Such leadership requires a chair who is appointed by God, gifted with integrity, trust and humility, and anointed by the Holy Spirit.

With understanding from spiritual discipline and insight from personal experience, David McKenna leaves no doubt. Unless chosen by God, the chair will fail; unless gifted with integrity, trust and humility, the board will fail; and unless obedient to the Spirit, the ministry will fail. Loud and clear, the message is sent to every Christ-centered ministry: The call of the chair is the call of God.

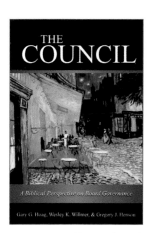

The Council: A Biblical Perspective on Board Governance
by Gary G. Hoag, Wesley K. Willmer, and Gregory J. Henson

This book seeks to answer the question, "What does the Bible say about board governance?" because followers of Jesus Christ who serve in board governance settings must start with the Scriptures. The Council offers an insightful, in-depth study of four governing bodies or "councils" that appear in the biblical record. By examining these historical accounts, we gain new perspective on how to think about board governance and how not to think about it. The book then goes on to present a logical, practical analysis and application of the biblical framework for governance that will impact the trajectory of your board for God's glory.

Available at ECFAPress • ECFA.org/ECFAPress